For Jude,

    a Good f

you enjoy the book.

        Prue

These Vagabond Shoes

THESE VAGABOND SHOES

PRUE CORLETT

ROBERT HALE · LONDON

ISBN 0 7090 6900 6

Robert Hale Limited
Clerkenwell House
Clerkenwell Green
London EC1R 0HT

A catalogue record for this book is available from the British Library

2 4 6 8 10 9 7 5 3 1

Typeset by
Derek Doyle & Associates, Liverpool.
Printed by
St Edmundsbury Press Limited, Bury St Edmunds
and bound by
Woolnough Bookbinding Limited, Irthlingborough

For my mother

I would like to thank all my family and friends for their support and encouragement. It was their enthusiasm for my story and their faith in my ability as a writer that convinced me to persist in my search for a publisher. I would also like to thank my publishers for all the help and advice I received.

Contents

Prologue

Since moving onto the boat I've started dreaming again. Maybe I was never suited to living in a house. Or perhaps it's the rocking motion that churns them out, although I don't remember having any difficulty before Peter died. Mind you, the dreams are usually disconnected and slightly bizarre – apart from last night when it was different. It was exactly like life. So much so that I knew I was awake and Peter was still alive.

We were back in the cave in Siracusa. Not our own cave but the big one we had stayed in when Peter first brought me to Sicily. We must have been celebrating Christmas or New Year because there were bottles of sparkling wine on the table and we never drank that normally. Everyone was there, Bernd, Wolle, Uwe and the rest, even Otto. I was surprised since Brindisi was his usual habitat whenever he was in Italy. Mario was playing his guitar and we were in full voice. The cave echoed with songs and laughter and the candlelight cast outlandish shadows on the rock walls. Otto was giving a tuneless blast on his kazoo and shouting across at me, his cheerful face flushed with beer and high spirits. 'Hey, lady, you are a vagabond now. Zis is ze life from ze street.' Peter had his arm round me and hugged me closer to him whispering in my ear, 'Baby-Prue, you looks so fucken good.' I think I must have felt the happiest woman alive to be leading such a free life with this unique man who loved me so passionately. And then I woke up.

I lay with my eyes closed and relived the scene, feeling cheated because I'd woken up so soon. I rarely dream of Peter and when I do I treasure it. I can see him still in my mind's eye. There he is,

9

sitting with his beard glinting red in the candlelight and his eyes twinkling at me, as blue as the summer sky. I can hear his voice too, deep and gruff with his quaint turn of English phraseology that so often caused a bubble of involuntary laughter to well up inside me – 'Baby-Prue, I been a little one drunking. But no problem.' Eight hilarious years on the road together and nothing had ever been a problem. Until the very end. Even then Peter accepted illness and death as philosophically as he'd accepted life. Many friends have died and many years have passed since then, and still I have only to glimpse a fleeting figure or hear the catch of a song and I'm back into that life that meant so much to us both. Such fun! I look back on those halcyon days and thank God that I have my memories. How dull life would have been if I'd never met Peter and been introduced to the freedom of a vagabond existence!

Prue Corlett
Hania Harbour, Crete
September, 2000

1   New Beginnings

It all started when I was fifty, when it suddenly hit me that I was middle-aged, recently divorced, I lived on my own and was beginning to feel that life would pass me by if I didn't take some action. My grown-up children, whom I loved dearly, were fully independent and I had no wish to burden them, in years to come, with feelings of obligation that they ought to visit regularly to make sure that I wasn't lonely or bored. I wanted to make an interesting life for myself, although I wasn't sure exactly what it was that I wanted. The only thing that I was certain about was that I didn't enjoy my highly stressful job with the Inland Revenue, I was weary of living in England and I longed for a bit of adventure. In my youth I had travelled a lot with my parents, never living in one place for long until I settled down to marriage and the rearing of my two children, and I suppose that now I was single again my innate wanderlust was resurfacing.

At any rate, after a lot of deliberation, I ignored all advice to wait until I reached pensionable age and decided to go abroad and do something completely different, giving in my notice to the Inland Revenue. I chose Greece as my destination because I'd been there on holiday and loved the country, and I was sure that with its thriving tourist industry I'd easily find a job to support myself. Also the cost of living was low and I had enough money saved to keep me going for several months should the need arise, and to boost my chances of getting work I took some Greek language lessons. I lived in rented accommodation with few possessions of my own beyond some personal junk which I deposited with my mother, so my biggest problem was to decide what I should take with me for an indefinite period abroad. In the end I bought a rucksack, which was more practical than a suitcase, and filled it with an assortment of clothes for every possible occasion, painting and writing materials, a travelling iron and my china figurine of the Japanese goddess of luck.

At last, full of self-assurance and excitement at the thought of the unknown, I flew into Corfu, an island new to me, lying green and enticing in the brilliant blue of the Mediterranean. I asked around for work and my initial confidence was amply rewarded when, within days of my arrival, I was offered a job in a pub. The only problem was that it soon became apparent that the owner expected more than my services in the bar. Concluding the deal, he offered me a beer and, to my acute embarrassment, casually started to stroke my jeans-clad thigh.

'Older women turn me on,' he said, smiling voluptuously. 'They appreciate good lovers and Greek men are the best lovers.'

I panicked. If I'd been quicker on the uptake I'm sure I could have produced a crushing response, but I've always been slow to react and by the time I think of a suitable rejoinder the appropriate moment has passed. As it was, crimson in the face and suffused by a hot flush, I slid off my bar-stool and croaked, 'I must rush! I've just remembered that my son's phoning me at my hotel. I'll see you later.'

I hastened out and went straight down to the port to find out when the first ferry to Igoumenitsa left the following day. I intended to be on it. It was a pity about the job but I really couldn't cope with a lecherous employer. The good thing was that at least it seemed clear that there was work to be found and I shouldn't have to worry in that respect, although my next job offer was no less traumatic.

I had answered an advertisement for bar girls in Messalonghi and was taken on with only the slightest hesitation with regard to my age. My employer impressed on me that Greek bars were nothing like English pubs and she expected her staff to mingle with the customers and go out of their way to be friendly. Her bar prices were expensive so there needed to be a particularly pleasant atmosphere, a point that seemed perfectly reasonable to me.

The pay was good, accommodation was provided and as I was naturally friendly, I had no qualms at all as I went out for the afternoon with Georgia, the young Greek girl who was to be my roommate. It crossed my mind that she was rather unsuitably dressed for the afternoon, wearing a skin-tight black mini dress with masses of make-up and jewellery but she had a charming manner and was obviously very popular with all the men we met. As was normal in Greece, there were very few women around in the afternoon.

A bulky, middle-aged man invited us to join him later for a coffee at his hotel, so after wandering around for a while, Georgia hailed a taxi and we drove to our rendezvous. She hadn't let me pay for a thing so far. We found the man without difficulty and after asking all the usual questions that one expects in Greece, such as was I married, how old was I and how much money did I earn, he and Georgia left the lounge together, relinquishing me to the company of a swarthy individual who looked not unlike a gorilla and introduced himself as Adonis. Without preamble, he suggested that we go to his place for a cup of coffee and a 'fiki-fiki' and he would give me 5,000 drachmas. The word 'fiki-fiki' was one that I hadn't come across in my BBC language course and I didn't much like the sound of it.

'No thank you,' I said politely.

Adonis looked astounded by my reply and explained that 5,000 drachmas was the standard price and I could hardly expect more. I could feel myself turning scarlet as I was enveloped in a mortifying hot sweat at the realization of what was expected of me. I reiterated my refusal and turned away, gazing stonily into the middle-distance and uncomfortably aware of the sudden buzz of conversation that had erupted round me while Adonis discussed my odd behaviour with the other men who'd been listening in. I was highly relieved when Georgia came back and we were able to go home.

This experience had completely put me off the idea of working in a bar and the following day, after an embarrassing evening spent hiding behind the sink and washing glasses, I went to Antirrio and took the ferryboat across to the Peloponnese.

13

I stayed at the youth hostel in Patras, intending to spend only one night there before going on to Athens. In fact I stayed a lot longer. Although the town itself struck me as being scruffy, dirty, untidy and polluted by heavy traffic, there was something very relaxing about the youth hostel with its rambling garden where I could sit all day writing or painting and chatting with other back-packers. They were mostly young and streetwise, and I loved listening to the stories of their travels and where they lived, and I decided to set my sights further than Greece and work my way around the world. After a few beers it all seemed so easy. Theodoro and his wife, Dana, ran the hostel and perhaps because their three children were so often around, the atmosphere was more like a home than anything else, always welcoming and friendly. A friend of theirs, Yianni, worked the night shift and when he heard that I was looking for a job, he said that he would keep his eyes open for me. True to his word, one evening before work he took me out to an ouzerie and introduced me to a man called Dimitri, an affable extrovert with a constant supply of jokes, who owned a restaurant and was looking for a waitress. He arranged to meet the next day and I set off eagerly for my appointment.

Dimitri greeted me enthusiastically and told me that the job would start in two weeks time when the tourist season got underway. Then, business over, he got us each a beer and launched into an account of his travels as a youth when he'd been in the merchant navy. He spoke in Greek, his English being very limited, with much laughter and gesticulation, describing the girls at the different ports of call, what services they provided and how much they charged, bemoaning the fact that one had to be so careful these days, what with AIDS being such a hazard. I remained silent and was careful not to join in with his laughter, but during the whole of this one-sided conversation he had given no hint of lechery towards me. When I got up to go, however, he cheerfully suggested a quick 'fiki-fiki' behind the counter first. This less than delicate approach would have struck me as funny if it had been directed at anybody else, but I was beginning to hate this preoccupation with sex and it must have taken several minutes of angry argument on my part before Dimitri could be persuaded that not all foreign women were looking for Greek men. Anyway, as far as I was concerned another job offer had disappeared down the drain and I was no further forward than when I had arrived in the country. It was time I moved on again.

But I was in luck because a friend of Yianni's telephoned that evening to say that there was work on a campsite in Kato Ahaia, about twenty kilometres outside Patras. I took the bus out there next day and introduced myself to the owner of the campsite, a humourless man who informed me that the job in question entailed cleaning the toilets and showers in the morning and working in the kitchen in the evening. Board and lodging were free and the wage was 1,500 drachmas a day. I was very taken with the campsite, which was huge and full of all sorts of shrubs and trees, beyond which lay a sandy beach. With an open-air restaurant shaded with rush matting and overlooking the sea, it looked so lovely and peaceful that I accepted the job on the spot.

Arriving at the campsite I was taken straight to my sleeping quarters, a little tent in which I thankfully dumped my rucksack before reporting for duty. My boss called himself Mr Basil and he introduced me to his grim-faced wife, Mrs Helen. Why it is that Kirios Vasilis and Kiria Eleni sound perfectly acceptable, but translated into English as Mr Basil and Mrs Helen, the names sound faintly comical? It has to be said that after the Inland Revenue the manual work on the campsite seemed like a holiday. I loved living in a tent, I loved the company of my youthful fellow workers and I felt healthier than at any time in my life. I even got pleasure out of my labours; not the cleaning in itself (does anyone enjoy scrubbing toilets and unblocking plugholes?) but in trying to finish everything in the short time I had. My legs lost their flabbiness, my skin had never been so clear and although not deeply brown, I acquired a healthy tan through swimming every day. But Mr Basil and Mrs Helen were not the easiest of employers, and although they treated me with a certain amount of courtesy, this wasn't extended to the younger workers, who left one after the other until I was working more or less on my own. When, in September, I was offered a job as cook in a taverna in the village, I accepted with alacrity.

My new bosses were Taso and his wife, Toula, and working for them was a completely different experience to my job on the campsite. They were both young and full of fun and treated me as one of the family rather than as an employee. The taverna opened at six o'clock in the evening and usually there would be a fairly steady stream of customers till about eleven, after which the bar would start to get busy, but although I was kept occupied grilling the meat, frying the chips and preparing salads, I was never rushed off my feet. I had to do the washing up and cleaning of the kitchen myself, of course, but if I was still working after half past eleven, Toula would come down to the kitchen and order me to stop doing whatever I was doing and join them at the bar – the cleaning could wait till morning. I was always kept well supplied with free beer or anything else I wanted, I could eat whatever I liked (on the campsite we existed on a diet of mainly cold stuffed tomatoes or cement-textured pastitsio – a kind of Greek lasagne), and I was paid the same wages as before. I loved it!

Eventually my job at the taverna came to an end when Taso closed down at the end of the season and I went back to Patras to prepare to go grape-picking. Never having done it before and having no idea how to go about finding work, I was glad to be joined by two young Geordies whom I met in the youth hostel, and we made our way to Nemea, one of the principal wine districts. It was a friendly little town in the mountains south of Corinth, where almost all the workers were foreigners, like us, who lived on a free campsite in happy camaraderie. Having no tent, we were offered the use of a derelict building and a Polish girl lent me a blanket as I had no sleeping-bag. I was slightly disappointed to discover that grape-picking was not as depicted in films, with grapes hanging conveniently at shoulder-height so that one skipped along airily tossing the bunches into baskets. It was hard work. The grapes grew at waist-height, causing a lot of back problems, and it was impossible to avoid getting one's fingers nicked by the sharp knives with which we were issued. But the workforce was comprised of cheery young students, we got a delicious midday meal of cold meat, salad, lemonade or wine, and the wage was 4,000 drachmas. I didn't complain.

For two days the sun shone and the nights were balmy, but then it started to rain and the temperature dropped so drastically that my Geordie friends and I found it hard to keep warm, having foolishly decided to travel light and leave most of our clothes back at the youth hostel in Patras. After ten days of sporadic work and continuing cold the three of us decided we'd had enough. We went back to Patras, where we parted company, the two men catching the ferry to Italy while I returned to the youth hostel for a few days of relaxation before going back to England to see my family.

It was at this point that I first met Peter. He was rather drunk at the time, roaring with laughter and teasing me unmercifully in German as I sat there quietly trying to bring my diary up to date. When I looked up and said politely 'I'm sorry but I don't speak German', he laughed all the more raucously and bought me a beer. Then another German, also happily inebriated, came up and sat down at the table.

Otto

'Hello, Mary-Lou,' he announced. 'I am Otto and zis is my friend Peter. We are vagabonds.'

Thus we were introduced! I saw a lot of them over the days that followed since I spent so much time in the hostel garden, as they did themselves. Otto did most of the talking (indeed, it was difficult to get a word in when he was around), but he did speak fairly good English. It was Peter, however, who attracted me. He was the taller of the two and very thin, with a bushy, reddish beard and penetrating, startlingly blue eyes. Sometimes I could feel him watching me but when I looked up he would turn away, embarrassed. In contrast to our first meeting he seemed a quiet and thoughtful character, but his English was so limited that usually Otto had to translate anything that he wanted to say to me. I learned that Peter had been travelling for twenty years, Otto for ten, and although they went their own ways, their paths would cross from time to time and they would travel together for a while. The day I left Patras, Otto told me that Peter was in love with me.

'Hey, lady,' he said, 'come on ze road wiz us. Zis man,' (pointing at Peter who was nodding his head vigorously) 'he will make all sings for you. Wiz him you will be OK. Hey, lady, he is a good man.'

Peter

I was sorely tempted, but common sense told me that the language barrier would prove to be too much of a problem since humour is important to me and I could neither speak nor understand any German at all. To have Otto translating for us would be most unsatisfactory, apart from the fact that I had already found that his extreme exuberance could be exhausting after a fairly short time. Regretfully I declined their offer but added, mainly for Peter's benefit, that I'd be coming back the following year and I hoped we'd meet again then. Peter shook his head.

'I go to Indian, baby, but make good you. My heart is full for you.'

It was the first time I'd heard him speak a full sentence in English. He hugged me close as we said goodbye and I wondered if I'd made the right decision.

2 Peter

Two months later I was back in Athens. While I was in England I did temporary work at the Inland Revenue to boost my finances and knew at once that I'd made the right decision in leaving, though I thoroughly enjoyed the company of my family and friends. Nevertheless, I yearned to be on the move again and couldn't stop thinking about Peter and wondering if by some chance he might still be in Patras. It seemed unlikely as from what Otto had said they never stayed long in one place, but I was eager to get back to Greece in any case. I had been promised work in a potato-sorting factory and I thought that if I could save enough money for a return ticket to Israel, I might be able to bluff my way into a job on a kibbutz.

In November it had been so balmy in Athens that I automatically assumed that the weather would be more or less the same throughout the winter, and it came as a shock to discover that Greece in the wintertime was bitterly cold, the marble tiling everywhere and the inefficient (or non-existent) central heating usually making it necessary to wear more clothes inside a house than outside. I arrived at the youth hostel in Patras to find Yianni already on duty, sitting behind the counter with a broad grin on his face and well wrapped up in a coat, scarf and woolly hat. He was delighted that I'd bothered to come back and got me a beer. I asked casually if Peter or Otto were still in Patras and he told me that they'd left only a few weeks previously but he had no idea where they'd gone.

Disappointed, I stood at the counter while we chatted about the things that had happened during the summer and I told him of my plans to go to Israel, which he considered most unwise in view of the political situation. Our discussion was interrupted by the sound of feet stamping up the front steps and the door burst open, letting in a blast of cold air. I gasped. It couldn't be! It was! With hair and beard both neatly trimmed, Peter stood there staring at me out of his forget-me-not blue eyes, astonishment and delight on his face. He dropped his rucksack and threw his arms out to me.

'Baby!' he shouted. 'You been here! Oh, Baby-one!'

I needed no invitation but rushed into his open arms and was enveloped in an almighty bear hug. Talking and laughing together I suddenly realized that without Otto, Peter seemed to be very much more forthcoming, although his English was rather confusing and spoken with a thick and unidentifiable accent. We sat on the stairs drinking beer till Yianni went to bed, whereupon Peter told me that he'd never stopped thinking about me since the day we'd first met and feared that he'd lost me for good. He was a difficult man, he said, but he genuinely loved me, and if I'd go to Italy with him he would never let me down. I was totally smitten and said 'yes' without a second thought. I had no idea whether it was fate or mere coincidence that had brought us both back to Patras three months to the day when we'd first met, but it seemed as if I was being offered a second chance and I intended to take it. I knew with an absolute clarity of mind that I was doing the right thing in spite of knowing so little about Peter. As we talked until the early hours of the morning, his heart seemed to reach out to me and awaken in me a passion that had for too long lain dormant. There was something about him, in contrast to his almost fiercely piercing eyes and prematurely wrinkled face, that exuded kindness and understanding. We were soulmates, we needed each other, and it wasn't simply a carnal desire that we knew would soon be satisfied; it was the feeling that we both had of having found the pot of gold at the end of the rainbow.

Our only remotely common language was English, which I had to speak slowly so that Peter would understand. I learned that he was bilingual in German and Italian, and also spoke very bad French, which he'd had to learn when he served in the French Foreign Legion. But he had a wonderful way with English, which

22

was liberally scattered with foreign words, incorrect words and swear words and which was almost impossible to listen to with a straight face. He also had a robust sense of humour. We were both born in September and it didn't bother Peter at all that I was thirteen years older than he was.

Next morning Peter told me that he was going to Rio to 'make shiffs' (which I assumed meant doing odd jobs on the ferryboats) and that in two or three days he should be able to save the money for our tickets to Italy. I didn't like to be totally dependent on him, however, and explained that I had enough money to pay for myself, which seemed to surprise but cheer him. I spent the day in Kato Ahaia visiting friends that I'd made in the summertime and when I got back to the hostel Peter was full of beer and exuberance. He told me proudly that he'd worked well and expected to have the ticket money for a boat leaving for Italy the following evening – if I wanted. He suddenly sounded anxious, taking my hands in his and gazing earnestly into my eyes as he asked me if I was sure that I wanted to go to Italy with him, saying that he was an alcoholic, 'a fucken problem man', and normally no woman could stay with him for long.

'But I love you, Peter,' I said. 'I won't leave you.'

To my amazement there were tears in his eyes as I smiled and kissed him.

The next day, when Peter came back from Rio, we bought our boat tickets, stocked up with plenty of beer and food for the voyage and after saying goodbye to Yianni we took the overnight ferry to Bari. It was a long and tedious journey. The ship's video wasn't working and it was the first time that I'd spent so long in Peter's company alone, but we got on as if we'd known each other all our lives and the hours flew by. He told me a lot about himself, although he was reticent about his childhood. I gathered that he'd spent many years in an institution, but when he was eighteen he'd gone to Sicily, where he began his 'street' life and then worked on a farm for a while. He talked a lot about the seven years he'd spent in the Foreign Legion, relating the most hilarious stories and making it sound like a boyish escapade, even though in reality the life must have been a hard one. He'd been in jail too ('I war a big fucker') and had got married once but, like me, he was now divorced. He obviously had an enormous zest for living life to the full and making the most out of any situation he was in, but he said that it was impossible for him to remain for too long in one place.

'I loff the life,' he told me simply, 'but I been a vagabond.'

At last we arrived in Bari and changed the last of our money into lire before going into the old part of the town to look up some friends of his. We stopped at various bars and wine houses where everyone seemed to know Peter and greet him with gusto and affection, buying us beer after beer until I was desperate to relieve my bladder. The worst of it was that none of these places seemed to provide a toilet, a state of affairs that I soon realized was commonplace in southern Italy. I suppose the men lived close enough to their drinking dens for it not to matter, or perhaps they found a quiet corner and peed up against the wall like they do in France, but for me the solution wasn't quite so simple. Peter sympathized and hurried me from one bar to another until at last we found a place where the barman reluctantly produced a key and led me to the back regions of the establishment. There, to my inexpressible joy, was a toilet with a notice on the door saying 'Out of Order' in Italian. It wasn't. Moreover it was spotlessly clean and when I came out I felt as if I were floating on air, so great was the sensation of relief.

While we'd been rushing about, Peter had noticed several posters advertising the Embell Riva circus, for which he had once worked, and he suggested that we go along to have a look as it was possible that we could get jobs for the wintertime. He discovered that the circus site was a long way from the centre of town and it was rather late by this time, but even if we missed the performance we'd be bound to meet someone he knew. So we set off at great speed and just as the colourful Big Top came into view he suddenly caught sight of a friend of his sitting in a restaurant on the other side of the road. We crossed over and, already beaming with pleasure, he took me inside.

'Matouche!'

'Pietro!'

The two men embraced affectionately and we were invited to sit

24

down and have some wine. Matouche was a midget, Yugoslavian, with a handsome face and hard grey eyes, and he and Peter reminisced over old times, exchanging news in a mixture of German and Italian. I understood scarcely a word, but Peter told me afterwards that there were jobs going in the publicity department and Matouche had suggested that we apply. What did I think? Did I like the idea?

I was intrigued by the notion of working in a circus but I was a bit apprehensive because I couldn't speak Italian, a hindrance that Peter brushed aside with an airy wave of the hand and a 'no problem, Baby'. By this time we were back in the town centre and sharing a beer in the railway station, where we had left our rucksacks. From under his tufty eyebrows, Peter looked at me across the table with an expression of amused embarrassment on his face as he confessed that he couldn't remember my name and that was the reason he always called me 'Baby'. I burst out laughing and told him, and from then on I was 'Baby-Prue'. I found out in due course that whereas his memory for wine houses was instinctive, his memory for names was appalling. It was now very late and the station bar was about to close. Peter told me that we would have to sleep outside as, having spent so much in the various bars, we were short of money and the friends with whom he had hoped to stay were no longer in Bari. It was no problem, however, as he knew of a good sleeping place which was out of the wind. This turned out to be the alcove outside a church, where Peter left me on my own to nervously guard our rucksacks while he went off in search of 'cartons'. Ten minutes later he was back with a large load of cardboard boxes which he flattened out and arranged neatly on the marble floor to form a good-sized base to insulate us against the cold. There we curled up together, sleeping like a pair of dormice until the cleaner woke us in the morning and asked us to take away the cardboard boxes, which we did.

We had our breakfast coffees in the station, mainly because there was a toilet there and I was able to wash and clean my teeth, and afterwards we walked to the circus site to find out if there were any jobs going as Matouche had said. We were in luck, because the Sikh who was in charge of the circus publicity was due to return to

India shortly and no replacement had been found. Peter had done this job before and was immediately taken on, with me to help distribute the advertising leaflets in the shops. Until these jobs became vacant we were to be general helpers, for a joint wage of 300,000 lire per week which would be increased when we started work in the publicity department. In fact, the promised increase was never to materialize, but we didn't know that at the time and the money seemed perfectly adequate to us.

We walked back into the old part of the town and, as we had very little cash left, Peter took me to what he called the 'Mensa', a free canteen for those in need. He explained that almost all Italian towns had one, usually run by the church, and that normally there was a place where people could get clothes as well, secondhand and completely free.

There was a varied assortment of characters eating in the canteen, mostly perfectly respectable-looking Italians and some Arabs. There were a few who seemed seedier, not badly dressed but excessively fidgety and restless and Peter told me that they were junkies. Our meal was delicious, I thought, pasta in a tomato sauce, a large piece of chicken, a side salad and coffee with an apple to finish up with. Peter gave me his apple, explaining that he couldn't eat it as he had no teeth. Not having noticed such an obvious defect, I thought he was joking until he opened his mouth obligingly to prove his point. Chuckling at my astonished expression he went on to tell me he'd 'killed' his teeth during army manoeuvres with the Legion, and that was why he now wore a beard.

We wandered to one of the public gardens where Peter had a siesta on a bench in the sun. I found it impossible to even doze while in the public gaze, so I wrote up my diary and amusedly contemplated his rather comical revelations until he awakened. After a refreshing cup of lemon tea, we wandered round to his friend's wine house to spend the rest of the evening, finally going back to the station to collect our rucksacks and use the station toilets before retiring to bed for our last night in the church alcove.

We were allotted a little cabin in one of the huge articulated trucks which were divided into about six similar compartments and, as

Peter was needed for work right away, I spent the morning trying to clean our living quarters. They had been occupied previously by two Indians, and it was evident that cleaning had been considered unimportant because everything was coated in a thick layer of grease and dust and the cooker was black with burnt-on food and oil. It was a small enough area to clean, having only a pair of bunk beds, a cupboard under the cooker, a table and chairs and a radiator, but it took me all morning to get it into a habitable state and I never had time to start on the cooker. In addition, there was the ever-present problem of a lack of toilet facilities and, by the time Peter had finished his morning's work, I was thoroughly fed up. By some instinct he had anticipated my needs and brought me a bucket which he had acquired from the elephants' tent, so my immediate problem was solved, but on a long-term basis I wasn't sure whether I could stand living in a country in which every bar did not have a usable toilet. To someone who hasn't suffered this inconvenience it may seem trivial, but I assure the reader that for a person of no fixed abode, especially for a woman, the situation can be a major problem, made even worse in my case because I was going through the change of life with all its embarrassing side effects.

We had lunch in the circus canteen with the Arab workers, a cheerful and noisy crowd of men who joked continuously with Alex and Luci, the two homosexuals who worked in the kitchen. Peter had to go back to work directly after lunch so I wandered round the site looking at the animals, getting into conversation with a beautiful Tunisian girl called Leyla who had a tiger-cub in her care, a mischievous little creature that had been born in the circus and wasn't yet old enough to work. Leyla spoke French and lived with her husband in a cabin like ours, he being a mere worker who, like Peter, didn't qualify for a proper caravan. The artistes lived in caravans with toilets and showers, in most cases their own property since the circus was their only life, but the labourers were, in general, a less permanent workforce. I asked the girl, in my halting French, how she coped without a toilet since she'd been with the Embell Riva for several months, which seemed an awful long time to have to make do with the limited facilities in Italy. She smiled wryly and told me that she got round the problem with a bucket or a plastic bag as she had no other choice, admitting that it was a less than satisfactory solution. However, I thought that she sounded eminently sensible and resolved to do the same thing, which put me in a much more cheerful frame of mind when I joined Peter for our dinner in the circus canteen.

Peter had only one spare set of clothes, so the next day he sent me to the church by the Mensa in the old town to get some more 'dresses' for him. He told me that the Sister in charge knew his size and wrote her a note in Italian with a list of his needs, drawing a detailed map for me so that I wouldn't get lost in the maze of little alleys. I found the place without too much difficulty and was given all that was on the list as well as some warm clothes for myself, which the Sister decided I needed. We were now well set up for the winter and Peter was pleased with my success.

That was the last day in Bari for the circus, so in the evening I watched the final performance and was impressed with what I saw. It was better than any circus that I'd seen in England, and no sooner had the performance finished than the vast tent was taken down with the most amazing speed and efficiency. Peter had no time to eat in the canteen so Alex gave me some food in a plastic bowl and I took it back to our cabin, where we ate together when Peter had finished his work. Having cleaned the cooker at last, I was beginning to feel at home, especially as some considerate Indians had given us tea, sugar, a saucepan and a water canister to tide us over until we got our first week's pay.

The following morning the circus prepared to move out in a massive convoy and Peter sent me to chat with Leyla until he'd been told which truck he was to drive. I liked Leyla; she was so refined and intelligent and very patient with my efforts to speak French. She gave me a lesson in Italian, teaching me how to listen out for certain words and pointing out how similar to French the language was. We were interrupted by Peter coming to collect me for our drive to Matera, which was our next stop and turned out to be a much more attractive town than Bari, being smaller and prettier and set at the top of a hill.

When we arrived I went for a walk, not wanting to get in the way as everybody else seemed so busy in setting up all the tents. I got back at lunchtime and met Peter briefly in the canteen, but he had to work directly afterwards so I wandered around on my own, feeling very much at a loose end. I would have liked to help but there was nothing that I could do and eventually I went back to our cabin to practise my watercolour painting. Peter was still working by the time it got dark, so once again I collected our food ration from the canteen and brought it back for us to eat later. He turned up two hours afterwards, very hungry and tired out from the day's exertions, wanting only to eat and sleep. Unfortunately, one of the problems of living in these little cabins in the articulated trucks was that the partitions were so thin that one could hear clearly everything that was happening on either side. It was normal for the Tunisians on the left of us to talk, not only to each other, but to shout across our cabin to the Tunisians on our right, and quite often they would have sing-songs in Arabic, thumping an accompaniment on any handy pot or pan. I didn't mind the music but it irritated Peter.

The following day I was given the good news that my services were required in the canteen and I was delighted that I would be working at last. Alex was the chief cook, exceedingly humorous and forever trying to make me laugh, while Luci enjoyed telling me his problems and used to flatter me outrageously, saying that I was 'brava' and not 'bruta' like most of the other people in the circus. To begin with I only had to do the washing up and cleaning of the kitchen, but as the days went by I was needed earlier to help make the salads and dish out the pasta and bread. There was always pasta to start with, in some uninspiring sauce, with either chicken or eggs to follow but never red meat, partly because the latter was too expensive and partly because the canteen had to cater for such a variety of religions. There would be a green salad as well, invariably made with fennel, the Italian word for which, 'finocchio', was also the slang term for a homosexual, and this caused a great deal of ribald laughter in the canteen. Alex had always known circus life and was very competent and sure of himself, but Luci hadn't been there long and didn't like the coarse jokes of the workers, getting very depressed and frequently ending up in tears. I used to feel sorry for him because he was so extravagantly effeminate and got teased a lot as a result, but Alex told me that he brought his problems onto himself by flirting so blatantly with all the men.

As soon as lunch was over and I'd finished cleaning up the kitchen, Alex and Luci would produce a large bottle of wine and insist that I stay and share it with them so that they could teach me to speak better Italian, and we would spend the afternoon sitting in the canteen, joking and laughing till it was time to start cooking the evening meal. Since Leyla's brief lesson, my Italian was coming along nicely and I could understand a little more with every day that passed. I had to as, apart from Peter, I worked with nobody who could speak even a few words of English. Once I'd finished in the canteen I'd go back to our cabin to wait for Peter, as he worked longer hours than I did and hardly ever got back until the evening performance had started. As well as being the chief cook, Alex used to work behind the circus bar on most evenings, so Luci would be lonely and want my company, either to watch the performance or just to talk. It was difficult to make him understand that Peter and I saw so little of each other during the day that we wanted to be alone together when we got the opportunity.

Most of the labourers in the circus were from Tunisia and Morocco, and there were quite a few Indians too, although I saw less of them as the majority were unenthusiastic about Italian food and cooked for themselves. The circus was the biggest I had ever come across and it was owned by the Bellucci family; the mother and her three sons. 'Big Mama' was the overall controller, Armando ran the publicity department and was the business brain, Roberto trained and performed with the tigers and Mario worked with the elephants and horses. Armando was my favourite out of the three brothers, always well mannered, genial and unflustered, and Mario was a romantic-looking and pleasant young man with whom all the girls fell in love. Roberto seemed a very much less cheerful character, positively surly at times and, although Peter told me that he worked far longer hours than anybody else in his efforts to ensure that the animals were well cared for, I saw no reason why his love for animals should excuse his frequent rudeness when dealing with lesser mortals such as ourselves. The other artistes came from all over Europe and included a couple of English dancing girls and an English clown. I had very little to do with the artistes as they lived in their own caravans and never ate in the canteen, but the few I did meet were always very friendly.

When I first started work in the circus I feared that I might find it difficult to accept that the animals were caged, but Peter explained to me that they were all born in captivity and knew no other life. I had to admit that they were all in beautiful condition and seemed perfectly contented, and I believe that animals that are kept occupied, either working or performing, are happier than those kept only for show purposes, and in some cases they may be even happier than house pets. The Embell Riva had a vast menagerie of elephants, tigers, horses, dogs, bears, a rhino, a llama, a baby giraffe and a Shetland pony. The last two were close friends, always housed next to each other and would perform in the ring only if they were together. There were also some hens that came into the clowns' act. It must have cost an enormous amount of money to feed them all and I often wondered how the circus made enough to pay for everything. Apart from the food and wages, the site had to be paid for and the fees for the publicity were incredibly high.

I loved the atmosphere of the circus with its camaraderie and the diversity of smells and sounds. There'd be the spicy aroma of cooking mingled with the dungy smells of the animals and the earth, the occasional reverberating growls from the tigers' enclosure or the whinnying from the horses' tent and the humphing and trumpeting of the elephants. I loved the evenings in particular as the darkness added its own enchantment. There'd be the gaudy lights of the Big Top and the dimmer lighting shining out of the caravans and the animals' tents, and one had to walk carefully in the dark to avoid tripping over all the guy ropes and electricity cables. Costumes, more tawdry by daylight, became magical and bejewelled at night, and I loved listening to the music during the performances and getting to know which tune belonged to which act. To me, the very air of impermanence was exciting, knowing that next day, or next week, we'd be somewhere else.

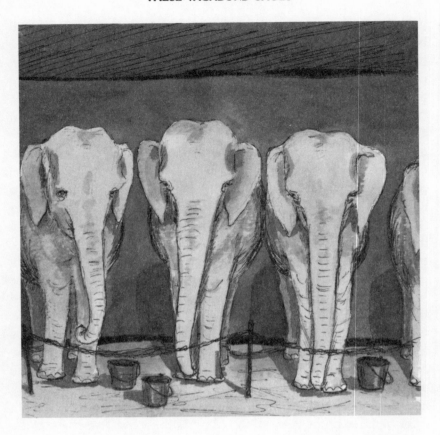

While we were still in Matera we were given our first week's pay and, after having begged, borrowed or done without, it was with a heady feeling of affluence that we went out to stock up with a few beers and other luxuries. We still ate in the canteen because I worked there, but Peter was bored with the monotonous diet and looked forward to taking over the publicity and being allotted our own caravan, where we would be able to cook for ourselves. However, the Indians who were returning home were not leaving the circus until it got to Andria and that was two weeks away.

At last we arrived there and the two Sikhs whom we were replacing returned to India, leaving their caravan for Peter and me to occupy. As should have been foreseen perhaps, it was incredibly grimy and needed two evenings of hard scrubbing with wire wool before it was presentable, but it was full of light from the many windows and was more spacious than the cabin. I washed the curtains and Peter painted the walls sky blue, with brown woodwork and, when we'd found a bit of old carpet for the floor, it was home. It already contained a double bed, an electric fire and refrigerator, a little gas cooker, a sink and numerous cupboards, although it lacked a toilet and a shower. By this time, however, I had developed the most amazing powers of water retention as well as being constipated for days at a time, besides which I had learned to improvise when necessary.

It seemed almost unbelievably peaceful to be at a distance from the incessant chattering of our cheerful but noisy Arab neighbours and from the sound of Arab music floating over the air day in, day out. And it was such a pleasure to have our own kitchen and to look forward to cooking what appealed to us instead of existing on the eternal diet of eggs or chicken, and fennel salad. But by far the most important thing for both of us was being completely alone together and experiencing the utter joy of having a measure of privacy in which to make love, a luxury which had been generally denied us in the cabin, the partitioning walls being so thin. We felt incredibly rich, as if we'd been given our own little world, away from circus life.

3   The Circus

Our jobs doing the publicity meant that we were advertising the circus in towns at least a week before it arrived, so when the circus was in Andria we had to work in Trani, the next but one posting for the Embell Riva. It wasn't far away so we were able to commute, leaving our caravan on the circus site. Peter was in charge, doing the driving, paying the fees in the municipal offices and selecting which posters to use and where to put them. They varied in size from one to twenty-four sheets, so it needed a practised eye to see which size would fit a particular spot and wherever there was a space there had to be a poster – bridges, hoardings, walls of every description, it had to be saturation coverage. Peter was working with a Sikh called Nasib, while I and another Sikh (whom Peter nicknamed Chiccio because he could never remember his real name) walked around the town sticking up leaflets in the shop windows and giving out cut-price tickets.

I loved the work. Peter would get me up at daybreak, making me coffee to bring me to life, as I was not a naturally early riser. Being February, it was bitterly cold in the mornings and Peter taught me to make hot red wine with a lot of sugar, which was a wonderful pick-me-up with which to start work on a winter's day. Peter and I would be ready to leave at seven o'clock but there would invariably be a delay while we waited for Nasib or Chiccio to do a last-minute chore, both of them seeming to get a kick out of postponing our departure and being masters of delaying tactics. At last we would be off, all four of us squashed into the front seat of the van with

Chiccio and I clutching our plastic bags full of leaflets, sellotape and cut-price tickets. The back of the van was full of the stuff that Peter and Nasib used, buckets of glue, brooms and masses of posters. Peter, normally so easy-going, became a different character once he was behind the steering wheel, tooting the horn furiously and hurling abuse out of the window at other drivers, sending us all into fits of laughter. We would arrive in the centre of town where Chiccio and I would be dropped off with instructions to rendezvous somewhere at about one o'clock, after the shops closed.

On my first day Chiccio decided that I would just accompany him into the shops to watch what he did, and the next day I would do the work while he looked on to make sure that I did it properly. In fact it was very simple. All we had to do was to go into each shop or bar, explain that we were from the circus and ask if we could put an advertisement in the window, after which we would graciously hand out a few half-price tickets. Peter told me that the circus never lost as only the expensive seats would be available, but it looked a generous offer and we were rarely refused. Chiccio, always jolly outside, had a surprisingly dreary way of introducing himself, his 'good morning' being delivered like an undertaker, his smile painfully false. Since I was enjoying myself I couldn't help asking him what was wrong.

'I don't like work,' he answered, unabashed.

He allowed me to stick the little posters in the shop windows and always checked my work methodically to make sure that I'd done it right, as if it wasn't a task that a child could do. He even walked slowly and showed enthusiasm only when we came to a bar, where he usually had a whisky while I worked, taking his time over it so that our passage along the street would be delayed. We met Peter at the appointed hour and all trooped off to a bar nearby, where we relaxed with a drink and a spot of conviviality. Peter was in very good form and regaled us with stories about other circuses he'd worked for, I joining in the laughter with the two Indians even though I couldn't follow all that he was saying, my Italian still being very limited.

Next morning it was my turn to do the business in the shops while Chiccio watched to make sure that I didn't make any drastic mistakes. Unlike him, I was full of enthusiasm and there was nothing gloomy about my 'good morning'. On the contrary, I thought I sounded like an advertisement for a bowl of sunshine cornflakes. People sometimes laughed at my imperfect Italian, but in a nice way and adding that 'piano-piano' I would become more fluent. I did everything without help and I knew that Chiccio was pleased with me because he soon stopped checking my handiwork and merely stood at the door, smiling benignly on the scene.

Peter said I was ready to work on my own next day so, as soon as the shops opened, Chiccio and I parted company and went in different directions. I had a wonderful time and found that when I was on my own the people in the shops were even more friendly and keen to talk and laugh than before. I was constantly being offered coffee or something to eat and questioned about the circus, about what animals we had and whether there were dancing girls and clowns. My progress was slow to begin with due to these unforeseen interruptions, but as the morning wore on and the shops became busier I was able to speed up, and by the time Peter picked us up I had distributed almost all my leaflets. Peter was proud of me, proud of the way I'd learned enough Italian to work on my own, and I basked in his compliments.

March came in, bringing with it the warmer weather, making work so very much more pleasant for all of us. It was never too bad for Chiccio and me, but Peter and Nasib had to work in the open air and relished the sunshine. We stayed with the circus all the way to Trani, and from there we commuted to work in the next two towns, Bisciegle and Barletta, but when Monopoli came up on the agenda, it was necessary for the publicity team to travel on ahead and park near the town as it was too far away for commuting purposes. Peter knew that I had a driving licence and asked me if I'd be willing to drive the van, towing our caravan, because he had to drive the big publicity truck (which housed the Indians as well as the bulk of the publicity materials), and it would save one of the other drivers from having to come out with us and find other transport back. I had never been a very good driver and I had never driven a van, let alone on the right side of the road, but Peter convinced me that it was perfectly simple. All I would have to do was to drive directly behind him and do whatever he did and then I couldn't possibly go wrong. He took me out in the van for a few lessons, wincing only when I strayed too far into the centre of the road or went too close to the kerb, but after a while I got the hang of it and considered that it wasn't as difficult as I'd expected and I'd give it a go.

The drive to Monopoli went without a hitch and the next journey, to Brindisi, was equally trouble-free, with me sticking as close to Peter's tail as was safe. My only problem was the presence of Nasib, whom Peter had decided should ride with me to give me a bit of moral support or help me if I got into difficulty. Unfortunately, he reeked of garlic and hardly stopped talking for long enough to draw breath, and I found the constant stream of chatter very distracting. On the drive to Lecce I asked him to be quiet so he started hawking and spitting out of the window, after which he began fiddling with everything on the dashboard and got seized by a violent fit of coughing. This was followed by more hawking and spitting and a spell of whistling tunelessly through his teeth, all the while fidgeting and fiddling with everything within reach. My nerves were getting frayed and to make matters worse, we arrived in Lecce in the middle of the lunchtime rush hour.

The circus site was on the far side of the town and although I did my best to stick behind Peter, I got stopped by a red light and two other cars got between me and his truck. I kept him in view and tried to catch him up at the roundabout by cutting in front of a bus, an unwise move which caused the bus driver to toot his horn furiously, attracting the attention of a policeman. I had no choice but to stop and endure a torrent of abuse in rapid Italian while Nasib sat there beside me, chortling with delight. Meanwhile Peter had stopped on the other side of the roundabout and walked back to the van to smooth things over. The policeman demanded to see my driving licence, which I produced and which was valid, but as it didn't bear a photograph of me the policeman refused to accept it and ordered me to accompany him to the police station. Peter produced his own, which was in fact simply a photocopy of a forged licence (he'd been banned from driving many years ago), but which bore a recognizable photograph. As far as the policeman was concerned that was perfectly in order and he was willing to accept Peter's word that mine was in order too. He also accepted two free tickets for the circus, had a laugh and a joke with Peter and waved us on our way with a warning to me to be more careful in future.

Our parking spot in Lecce wasn't the best we'd come across, being directly on a busy main road and opposite a school so that we got no privacy whatsoever. However, there was a bar where the friendly owner allowed us to use the toilet and fill up with water whenever we needed it in addition to which he gave us cut-price drinks. I liked Lecce. It was a big city but it was attractive, with tree-lined streets and a huge open-air daily market, and the people seemed particularly nice. Peter knew it well and sometimes after work he took me into the old part of the town to visit his favourite wine house, which was run by a relaxed character called Michele. The wine was good too, and Peter liked to sit and gossip with his Italian friends or play a few games of cards.

I'd been to wine houses with Peter in other towns and I always preferred them to the bars, mainly because it was possible to sit and drink, whereas in the vast majority of bars there were no tables or chairs at all, or if there were it would cost extra to drink sitting down. Accustomed as I was to the cafeneions (traditional coffee-houses) in Greece this system seemed highly unsociable. The only problem was that these wine houses were usually exclusively male domains, especially in the smaller towns and villages, so before bringing me inside Peter would ask, out of politeness, if there were any objections to my presence. It was important to him to have me by his side and he took obvious pleasure in my company which I found very flattering.

Although we both liked Lecce, where Peter's job was concerned it was not such a good town. In Brindisi the circus had been approached for extra insurance in addition to the advertising fees, and in Lecce it was the same, except that there the demand was less delicately made. On the first day that Peter and Nasib started work they were stopped at gunpoint by two policemen who demanded cash for each poster they put up. Peter explained that he and Nasib were only employees and the policemen should speak to the circus directors. Next morning Armando told him that an exorbitant 'donation' had been demanded and he had refused to co-operate, but Peter was to continue working normally as the legitimate fees had been paid and the posters were all correctly stamped. This was easier said than done because as fast as the posters were raised, the following day they would be covered up or torn down, this form of harassment continuing all the time we were in Lecce even though Peter regularly worked till midnight to foil the spoilers. As Nasib disliked going out at night, Peter taught me how to roll up the separate sheets of paper and hand them to him in the correct order and I went out with him instead. I loved our evening forays. I welcomed any chance to be with Peter and I felt proud to be helping him.

The job that Chiccio and I did was largely unaffected by this anti-publicity drive, and the shops and bars usually displayed our little leaflets, but when the circus arrived and performances commenced, Animal Rights protestors paraded up and down outside the Big Top and audiences were considerably less than they should have been for a town the size of Lecce. Roberto Bellucci thoughtlessly accused Peter of laziness and blamed the reduced audiences on the shoddy work of the publicity team. Peter was outraged and instantly resigned, storming off to the office to collect our pay and our papers. He was only dissuaded from leaving by the combined efforts of Matouche and Armando, who explained that Roberto had been unaware of the problems with the local Mafia, but that he would be enlightened immediately. When Peter had calmed down, I went over to the canteen to see everybody because it had been a long time since we'd stayed on the same site as the circus. I was greeted with cries of joy and hugged affectionately by Alex, who asked me coyly if I would go shopping with him next day to help him choose some new make-up. There was no sign of Luci and when I mentioned his name Alex pouted and called him a 'bastardo', going on to tell me that two days before, when he'd been given the money to buy the groceries for the kitchen, Luci had gone out and had not returned.

Later on, one of the workers reported seeing him in Brindisi railway station so it was assumed that he'd gone back to his home town of Manfredona. I wasn't surprised as Luci had never been happy and he was almost certain to have been owed money by the circus, anyway.

One of the less desirable aspects of circus life was that we nearly always had a problem in getting paid as the wages were taken out of the box-office kitty and, if the audiences were low, Peter would be told to come back another day. We were never less than a week behind, sometimes more, and although Peter was usually advanced the money for the advertising fees, he had to pay for the diesel and oil himself, the money for which would be reimbursed later. Peter told me that this was a problem common to most circuses and there were others far worse than the Embell Riva, but this knowledge didn't help when we were short of cash ourselves. I couldn't help feeling that this was a cunning ruse on the part of the circus directors to ensure that their workers stayed, because after being insulted by Roberto Bellucci I feel sure that Peter would have left if he had been paid in full.

Our next move was to Maglie which was only a little town and beautifully peaceful after all the action in Lecce. Peter parked at a garage conveniently situated halfway between the circus site and the town centre and we stayed there for two untroubled weeks. I could never understand why the directors so often picked the most one-horse towns imaginable unless it was to avoid problems with the Mafia, but Peter told me that the site fees were much lower in these places. I also found it puzzling why there seemed to be no proper advance plan for the circus, because although the big towns had to be booked well ahead, very often the smaller ones wouldn't have been decided upon until only a few days before the circus was due to perform. Mola di Bari was selected only the *day* before the arrival of the circus and it was too late for Armando to get a printer to do the data. Fortunately Peter used his considerable charm (and several free tickets) to persuade one firm to give the circus priority and the relevant data was printed, though we worked until three o'clock in the morning to get all the publicity done in time.

A part of my job that I didn't enjoy so much was having to prepare the big posters for Peter and Nasib. This involved opening and flattening out the huge rolls of paper, separating the sheets and then putting them together in such a way that each lot belonged to one particular poster. Then these would have to be folded in a special way so that not only would the top sheet be pasted up first, but the picture on the outside would indicate to what size of poster it belonged. Physically it was hard work, first flattening out the heavy rolls of paper and then getting down on hands and knees to do the folding. Once he'd taught me how to do it, Chiccio would absent himself during the opening and flattening process and reappear only in time to separate the sheets (the easiest part), leaving me to do the work on the ground. It annoyed me because he was a lot younger than I was, but try as I might to persuade him to let me separate the sheets once in a while, the only time he did the heavy labour was when one of the directors was in the vicinity.

I must say that although Chiccio was shamelessly lazy, he used a certain amount of charm and guile, frequently bringing me a cup of tea to keep me sweet while I worked. He amused me too much to allow me to feel aggrieved for long because he was such a jolly little man and I much preferred his company to that of Nasib who was irritatingly officious and forever trying to tell me how to do my job.

Both Indians took a delight in any mishap. Whenever the van broke down, which happened quite often as it was so old, Nasib would rub his hands together, chuckling with glee at the hitch in our routine, and both he and Chiccio had a habit of forgetting some vital item when Peter drove us to a supermarket, remembering it only when we were on our way home so that Peter would have to drive back. They regularly took advantage of his good nature, but the most galling aspect of it all was that they were both getting far higher wages than we were, our promised pay-rise never having been effected. It wasn't so much the money that bothered us, since we lived very well on our wage, but it was the unfairness of the situation. Peter worked far harder than any of us and it was important to him that he did a good job as he took pride in his work, but both

42

Indians did as little as they could get away with, and skived off duty whenever possible.

After Maglie we drove on to San Vito dei Normanni, the next tiny town on the agenda, and finished the advertising easily in one day. Ostuni came next but when Peter asked for the two weeks pay we were owed, plus the advertising fees, he was told that all the money 'in the kitty' had been paid out already, but Sergio, the accountant, would drive over from the circus the following morning to bring funds. He never arrived, though we waited all day with Peter getting more and more frustrated as the hours went by since Ostuni was a fair-sized town and he hated wasting time. When there was no sign of Sergio on the second morning, Peter said that he wasn't going to wait any more and would make the money himself by giving a fire-show. He was the man!

He had noticed posters advertising a festival in Carovigno, a little town on a hill not far from where we were parked, so he took us there in the van and, leaving Chiccio and Nasib to chat with the Indians at the funfair, went to the police station to ask for permission to give a fire-show. They were perfectly agreeable and we drove home in high spirits, all of us infected by Peter's enthusiasm. I was intrigued, never having seen a fire-show, and watched Peter's preparations with interest, the more so because he told me that I would have to go round with an old hat to make the collection. He rummaged around in his battered rucksack and found what he wanted: a couple of metal rods, some cotton wool and thread, and a crumpled yellow fakir's costume. Sitting on the step of our caravan, he bound a wad of cotton wool onto the end of each rod, made a few cotton wool balls, and broke up some empty beer bottles, putting the pieces in a plastic bag. He put his costume on under his normal clothes and we were ready to go, stopping off in Ostuni to buy some kerosene for his act.

We arrived in Carovigno at about eight o'clock in the evening and strolled hand-in-hand along the little precinct, looking at the stalls and keeping an eye open for a suitable place to put on his show. Peter found a convenient spot in front of a bar and we shared a few beers until the place began to fill up with people, at which point he decided that it was time for his show. As he laid out his apparatus a small crowd gathered, curious as only Italians can be, so when Peter took off his outer clothing and stood resplendent in his yellow costume and bare feet, his audience doubled almost immediately. He marked out the corners of a square with cotton wool balls, lighting them as he went, and then he introduced himself to the people and the show began.

After a moment of ceremonial ritual, he lighted his prepared rods so that they became flaming torches and spat sheet after sheet of flame into the air, causing a burst of excited cheering and clapping. He extinguished the fiery torches in his mouth and relit them, running the flames across his chest and up and down his arms, moving like some sort of a weird dancer. Then he emptied the broken glass onto the ground and walked, jumped and stamped on the jagged pieces while people clapped appreciatively. Calling for two of the biggest men in the audience, he asked them to stand on his back together while he lay chest down on the glass, getting to his feet afterwards and showing no signs of injury. He finished off his show with another fire-spitting display as I went round the enthusiastic crowd collecting money in the hat as they cheered and clapped and milled round him, asking umpteen questions. He chatted with them while he changed, and we shared a beer between us before picking up Chiccio and Nasib and driving home. Back in our caravan, he counted the money and found that we'd collected nearly 300,000 lire, almost as much as a week's wages.

Next morning he paid the advertising fees in Ostuni and we all worked hard and fast until the shops closed, driving home in a mood of elation after the two days of inactivity. We found Sergio waiting for us with a face like a thundercloud so Chiccio and Nasib scuttled off quickly to their quarters in the big publicity wagon. Without a word of greeting Sergio demanded to know if there was any truth in the rumour that Peter had been giving fire-shows and taking badly-needed audiences away from the circus. Peter demanded to know how he was expected to pay for the publicity without money and pointed out that the fire-show had been given in a small town where the Embell Riva had no performances booked. Still smarting from Roberto Bellucci's criticism in Lecce, he added that it was clear that his efforts weren't appreciated by the directors and therefore he would resign and collect our pay and our papers immediately. Sergio was shocked and became apologetic and conciliatory, but after going to so much trouble for the circus, Peter felt insulted and refused to be mollified. However, when we arrived at the office, Armando pleaded so charmingly for Peter to

45

stay on for a bit longer that he capitulated and agreed to stay till the end of the winter tour.

Our next stop was Termoli, several hundred kilometres to the north and in the direction of the circus headquarters. This time I insisted on driving alone as it was too far to go with the distracting presence of Nasib beside me, and he would be useless if any problems arose. Despite the most atrocious weather I arrived safely, but the next day when Peter was driving, the brakes failed, and the day after the battery died. I'd been lucky. Then Chiccio went back to India and the publicity department was reduced to three, although we seemed to get by with the minimum of problems.

The circus joined us in Termoli and once again I had a joyous reunion with Alex in the canteen, catching up with all the latest gossip and intrigues. Alex had the most wonderful way of turning the slightest incident into high drama, rolling his eyes and glancing from side to side as he related some story, putting his finger to his lips and telling me not to breathe a word to anyone else. Apparently, ever since Lecce, business for the circus hadn't been as good as had been expected considering that it had been the Easter season, but Alex told me that in his opinion the audiences hadn't been too bad for the size of the small towns they'd performed in. However, the box-office takings were down and, meeting Peter accidentally in a bar one evening, Roberto Bellucci sneeringly announced to all and sundry that since 'the great fakir' (indicating Peter) obviously made more money with his fire-show than the artistes in the circus, he would have to pay for everyone's drinks. Peter, taken aback at this uncalled-for display of spite, did so without hesitation, laughing and remarking flippantly how flattered he was that his one little fire-show in a town far from the circus site should have proved so successful that he had become a star overnight. His sarcasm sank in and from then on he and Roberto ignored each other completely.

We remained in Termoli to do the publicity for the little mountain towns of Guglionese, Larino and Atessa. These were pretty little places with narrow, cobbled streets and archways leading into flowered courtyards – not swamped by the modern high-rise architecture that kills the beauty of so many Italian towns, but at the same time not having the best circus sites for large audiences. Then May arrived and it was time to travel northwards to the circus headquarters near Lanciano where the final performances of the winter tour were to be held. There were several small towns and villages in the area where the circus would work for one or two days at a time, but none of the publicity data had been printed before we left Termoli, so when we arrived in Lanciano in advance of the circus we had two glorious days of relaxation.

The site covered a huge area with a large warehouse in which other trailers and caravans were stored and, to my immense gratification, there were toilets and some hot showers which we could use. Peter introduced me to a German friend of his, Vladimir, who looked old and distinguished, his long white hair topped by a fur hat and wearing a black velvet jacket. He had worked for a number of circuses in his lifetime and his speciality had been a high-dive act, the like of which had never been seen since he retired. He lived permanently on the site with two old Frenchmen, one in a wheelchair, all of them semi-retired, and no sooner had we arrived than we found ourselves sitting in the sunshine with them and drinking beer together. We talked in a strange mixture of languages, French, German, Italian and even the odd word in English. Vladimir had worked with Peter many years before, doing the publicity for the Embell Riva, but mostly he reminisced about his days as an artiste, every now and again bursting out with the introduction to his act, 'ra-ta-ta-ta – and *now*, ladies and gentlemen – *Vladimir* – the lion of *Russia*.' He asked Peter if he ever wanted to go back to his high-wire act, Peter having apparently once been a tightrope walker with a troupe of German artistes.

'You never told me about that,' I complained, and Peter waved his hand dismissively, telling me that maybe we'd come across them some time but that he had no intention of working 'in the sky' again. He'd lost his nerve.

For the rest of that day and the next we had an easy, peaceful time, going out only to stock up on groceries and quantities of beer, as Vladimir and both the Frenchmen congregated outside our caravan for impromptu chat sessions. But then the circus arrived, wagon after wagon and caravan after caravan rolling in and destroying the tranquillity of the place with the normal hustle and bustle of workaday life. On the days that followed we did the publicity in Lanciano and the surrounding towns with Nasib becoming increasingly difficult to work with. He was convinced, for some obscure reason, that he would be the next head of the publicity department and swaggered around trying to give us orders and becoming aggressive if Peter put him in his place.

On our last day with the circus, the three of us went out in the van to do the advertising for Guardiagele, a remote little town in the mountains, and on the way Nasib became so truculent and bossy that Peter threatened to leave him on the roadside if he didn't keep quiet. He immediately started to get abusive and insulting so Peter stopped the van and ordered him out, driving off and leaving him in the middle of the road shouting and shaking his fists at us. He did deserve it and I couldn't help laughing, but at the same time I felt that Peter was a bit extreme in his treatment. He grinned and told me not to worry because Armando was coming along any minute with the newly-printed data and he'd take Nasib home.

Sure enough Armando caught us up and asked what the Indian was doing on the roadside on his own. When Peter told him the story, he burst into roars of laughter and agreed to pick up Nasib and take him back to the circus, provided that Peter was certain we could manage all the work on our own. We worked hard and fast, pausing only for beer and a snack and doing without our siesta. Peter wanted to prove that not only could we work efficiently by ourselves, but the publicity would be even better than before. It was late in the evening by the time we'd finished and the van broke down on the way home. This was normal, of course, but Peter coaxed it back to life and we chugged back to the circus at about ten kilometres an hour.

When we arrived at the office to collect our documents and our pay, everyone was eager to hear the story of why Nasib had been dumped by the roadside and their grins turned to explosions of laughter and in the hilarity that followed it was generally agreed that such treatment should have been meted out a long time before. We sat and talked for a while longer and then left to say goodbye to Matouche and Alex before going back to our caravan to pack. As we went to sleep for the last time in the little caravan that had been our home for what seemed so long, I felt quite sad at the thought of leaving. Circus life may have had its problems but it also had an *esprit de corps* that I'd never found in ordinary life.

4 Frivolous Summer Days

We had decided to spend the summer in Greece, and with money in his pocket Peter wanted to go to Naples to buy a few things to sell if times were hard. Not far from the Central Station in Naples there is a rather scruffy area where one can buy cheaply almost anything one wants. The shops are full of factory surplus, factory rejects and maybe stolen goods as well, but as long as one checks what one buys it's possible to find the most wonderful bargains. Peter bought some attractive pocket watches, a few small radios and several yo-yos with flashing lights, and after the tastiest restaurant meal I'd experienced so far in Italy, we took the night train to Bari. I liked the town better this time, maybe because it was summer or maybe because I could speak the language better and was more sure of myself. We stayed there for two days, spending a lot of time with Peter's wine house friends, eating at the Mensa and sleeping under a palm tree in one of the public gardens. As Peter said, our millionaire days were over and we were vagabonds again.

We took the ferry to Patras where we checked into the youth hostel and Peter found work almost immediately painting houses for a friend of Theodoro. Unless I could get a morning job, he told me, he didn't want me to work as he wanted my company in the evenings and his wages were quite enough to support us. I wasn't quite as confident as he was but it gave me a chance to do my painting so I fell in with his plans.

We lived in what was known as the 'trailer', a big wooden shed full of beds and reserved for down-and-outs with little money, such as ourselves, or as an overflow if all the rooms in the hostel were

51

full. At that time only Peter and I were in residence and we valued this privacy even though the trailer was suffocatingly hot at times with only the door and one small window for air. We bought a little camping-gas cooker and if the meals we produced weren't as lavish as those we'd cooked in the circus, at least they were tasty and filling. Our funds were strictly limited, the main problem being the youth hostel bill which used to mount up at an alarming rate, but Peter was adamant that we could manage on his wages. The eternal optimist, he never worried about such trifles as bills when he had enough money on him to pay for food, beer and cigarettes.

Having tried unsuccessfully to get work during the day, I decided to get together enough watercolours to take up to Athens to sell. Unfortunately my style was very painstaking and slow, and I could never complete more than about three pictures in a day. It was a wonderful life for me of course, since while Peter was at work painting his houses, I sat in the hostel garden all day painting pictures, drinking beer and making merry with the other hostellers, many of whom were long-term residents like ourselves. They all loved Peter, with his raucous voice and refreshingly politically incorrect attitude to life, and after our evening round of cafeneions and wine houses we would always come back to drink a few beers with them, sitting outside in the fresh air and enjoying their company.

After a while I managed to accumulate a reasonable stock of watercolours as well as some miniature paintings on marble, and went up to Athens for the day, finding a convenient position in Monastiraki to sit on the pavement with my wares spread out in front of me. I should have taken a lot more money for the amount of pictures I sold, but being a hopelessly bad salesman, I was easily beaten down from my asking prices and felt ridiculously satisfied that I'd managed to make enough profit to pay for my trip as well as about half of the youth hostel bill. Eventually, however, as the bill continued to mount inexorably, I decided to take whatever job came my way. Being in debt bothered me as I hadn't yet acquired Peter's carefree philosophy of living for today and worrying about the morrow when it came.

So I took a job washing up in a restaurant almost opposite the hostel, more lucrative than my painting venture but with very unsociable working hours, from six o'clock in the evening until about two or three o'clock the following morning. It was a very happy atmosphere to work in, full of laughter and non-stop banter, and we were always so busy that the evenings flew by. However, the washing up in itself was less enjoyable because my supervisor would insist on adding to the water so much extra detergent, including soap powder and bleach, that within ten days the skin of my hands had become as hard and scaly as a reptile's. Peter hated my working there because we saw so little of each other, and when his own job came to an end he persuaded me to leave and go with him to Kefalonia, where a cafeneion friend had a restaurant and had promised him work. By this time we had actually managed to save some money – enough for the tickets with some left over – and as it was now almost September with little work to be found in Patras, I was happy to try somewhere else.

So we packed our rucksacks and made the three-hour ferry trip to the tiny port of Sami, from where we got a bus to the capital, Argostoli, and made enquiries as to the whereabouts of the address we'd been given. Kefalonia was a beautiful little island, green and mountainous and not as touristy as Corfu, and it turned out that Peter's friend lived in a little village outside Lixouri, which entailed another short ferry trip, followed by a taxi ride as we'd missed the last bus. It was after eleven o'clock in the evening by the time we arrived at the restaurant, but we received an affectionate welcome by Peter's friend, Dionysis, who treated us with typical Greek hospitality, plying us with food, beer, cigarettes and giving us a bed in his house. He seemed to have forgotten that he had offered Peter work and when Peter mentioned it, he laughed heartily and clapped him across the shoulders.

'You want work, my friend?' he shouted 'No problem! I know many people who can give you work. There will be much work for you tomorrow, for sure!'

He reminded me of a fat and jolly pirate with his thick, black beard, curly hair and rolling black eyes. He needed only an eyepatch and a parrot to complete the picture.

The next day we met the people from the village as they dropped into the restaurant throughout the morning for a drink and

53

a chat. Most certainly there was work, we were told, plenty of work, and it appeared that everyone knew somebody who needed workers. On learning that Peter could drive, one man told him that he needed a driver for his lorry and would return with it later in the day to give Peter a trial. Naturally we were both delighted, especially when Dionysis told us that he always spent the winter in Patras, so we could live in his house while he was away, for only a small fee. The evening came and yet more people dropped in for a drink of two, all very affable and encouraging, but the man with the lorry never turned up and nor did anyone else who could give us a concrete offer of work.

'No problem!' we were assured. 'If there's no work today there'll be work tomorrow, or after tomorrow. You have time! Take it easy!'

We did take it easy during the days that followed, but there was never any sign of work in the immediate future, always next day or next week, and to break the monotony one afternoon, a lad called Costa took us to the beach in his car.

'I am a very good swimmer,' he informed us. 'Also I can lift many kilos.'

He stripped down to his minuscule swimming trunks and spent a few minutes exercising in front of us, flexing his glistening muscles and inflating his bronzed chest. As soon as Peter and I were undressed, he sat down beside Peter and ostentatiously compared the size of his biceps to Peter's own.

'See that!' he said proudly, flashing me a broad smile through tobacco-stained and broken teeth. 'I can lift more kilos than anyone in my village.'

Peter caught my eye and exploded into laughter, covering up his amusement by hurrying down to the water and swimming rapidly out to sea. Costa immediately dived in and tried to catch him up, but Peter was by far the better swimmer and left him far behind. Undaunted, Costa turned back and bounded out of the sea to do press-ups on the beach in front of me, ending up with a perfectly executed handstand and leaping back onto his feet with a flourish.

'Bravo!' I applauded enthusiastically and got up, smiling, to go for a swim just as Peter came back. When I joined them later they were talking animatedly about motorbikes, a subject that kept them occupied till it was time to go home. As he dropped us off at the restaurant, Costa turned to me and said, 'Your husband is a very clever man. He knows all about motorbikes and he has ridden one in a circus. You are both good people.' We felt honoured by this unexpected praise!

We lingered on for a few more days, hoping that one of the jobs mentioned would materialize, but although everybody reassured us and told us not to worry, we were once again at rock-bottom financially and came to the reluctant conclusion that we could wait no longer. Peter was getting restless, besides which we didn't want to abuse Dionysis' hospitality, so we thanked him and took our leave, taking the bus back to Lixouri and thence to Argostoli.

We needed to make money quickly and found a shaded place outside a supermarket in the main street, spreading out what remained of my watercolours and marbles and hoping for the best. Peter found me a beer crate to sit on as well as a fresh piece of white marble to keep me occupied, and as I sat there and painted, he managed to sell two of my watercolours for double what I had been selling them in Athens. Now that we were solvent again he left me to go in search of a cheap place to eat and drink and a sleeping place for that night, and while he was away I sold one of my marble miniatures. He wanted to give a fire-show that evening but by the time it got dark, a strong wind arose and made it impossible for him to work. Keen to make money, he took my pictures and hawked them round a few restaurants, selling a further three watercolours and two pieces of marble, again for double the amount I had taken in Athens. We spent the night on the deck of a rusting and obviously disused fishing boat, on a pile of dry matting, sheltered from the wind and comfortable. It was still pleasantly warm and we slept like logs until being awakened by the lorries delivering fruit and vegetables for the market. I worked like a beaver all that day and the next, painting pictures outside the supermarket and occasionally selling one, although Peter sold the most by going around the restaurants in the evenings with them. Within a short time we had made the money for our tickets back to Patras, and we had also been living well and eating every day in a cheap restaurant. It looked as if Kefalonia was an island worth coming back to in the future.

Back in Patras we had a stroke of luck, as Dana, who did all the cleaning at the youth hostel as well as working in the reception and coping with her normal chores at home, was very overtired and asked me if I would do the cleaning of the hostel in return for free bed and breakfast for myself and Peter. I jumped at the chance as the youth hostel bill had always been our greatest problem and, compared to the cleaning I had done on the campsite, the hostel was child's play. It left me plenty of time to paint, but unfortunately, however hard Peter tried to sell my pictures, business in Patras was nowhere near as good as it had been in Kefalonia. His old employer was still away on holiday and even though Peter did odd jobs whenever he could get them, or gave a fire-show when the weather allowed, we were once more living from hand to mouth. The summer was over and he was eager to get back to Italy, but I wanted to stay till the end of October as my daughter was due to visit Patras on an inter-railing holiday. Peter pondered for a while and eventually suggested that he go back to Italy on his own to capitalize on the festival season in Pugha, during which it was possible to make a lot of money with his fire-shows.

Of course I agreed, since Peter clearly wanted to go and there was no point in wasting money on two tickets to Italy for such a short time, besides which I had my job in the youth hostel. I missed him at first after he left, but I was kept so busy with my work and had so many friends to socialize with that the days passed quickly, and it seemed hardly any time at all before he was back again. He arrived in style, moreover, on a little motorbike and with a wad of Italian lire in his pocket. He chuckled at my amazement, telling me that he had regularly given two fire-shows a night and after the first festival he had bought the motorbike very cheaply from a friend in Bari, subsequently using it to take him back and forth to the other festivals and recovering the money in less than a week.

Our peace was shattered a few days later when Otto arrived with several other German vagabonds and we were no longer on our own in the trailer. It was lovely to see him again as his exuberance was so infectious, but it wasn't long before we both began to tire of

56

his company. He'd bought himself a kazoo and played it loudly and tunelessly at all hours of the day and night, so that sleep was hard to come by, but at the same time it was nice for Peter to be able to reminisce with his old friend about their experiences on the road together. Some of these were so outrageous that had I not known the characters I would have found them incredible!

One of the people staying with us in the trailer at this time was a long, thin, middle-aged German named Hans. He had been very free-spending, buying beers regularly for all and sundry and chatting up the young backpackers, and one evening, in a fit of drunken generosity, he invited everyone in the hostel to a meal in the Chinese restaurant nearby. Money was no object, he insisted when Peter warned him that he'd picked one of the most expensive restaurants in Patras. He was a connoisseur of Chinese cookery and he wanted us all to sample its delights with him. None of the young backpackers wanted to join the party and the six of us who remained seemed unlikely clientele for such an exclusive establishment, and it must be said that we would have been perfectly happy eating souvlakis (meat-filled pittas) in the square. But Hans was adamant – he wanted to eat Chinese and he didn't want to eat alone.

So we all trooped off to the restaurant, which was one of the classiest in Patras with plush carpets, muted pink lighting and linen tablecloths, and as we entered in our habitual disarray, both customers and staff stared at us with a certain amount of trepidation. Hans, wearing a white sun-hat, was so tall that his trousers stopped well above his ankles, and Crooke, on crutches, wore army surplus fatigues which were far too big for him. Plump, balding Bobbish, with his high-pitched titter, had on a Fair Isle pullover in spite of the heat, while Otto, already inebriated and dressed in a singlet and shorts, marched in playing his kazoo. Peter and I, not renowned for our sartorial elegance or decorum, were comparatively sober and must have looked like pillars of respectability by comparison.

We were shown to a table but Hans waved away the menus and announced that he was well-acquainted with Chinese food and would order for us all. We would start with bird's nest soup accom-

57

panied by a bottle of Mateus Rose for himself and 'the lady', and good German beers for his friends. By the time the soup arrived Otto was in the blissful state of being able to communicate only with his kazoo, which made conversation rather difficult. He didn't want his soup so Bobbish and Crooke shared it between them, and as soon as the beer was finished another round was ordered immediately to go with the next course.

'Peking Duck!' shouted Hans. 'Six times!'

The waiter looked worried and went to speak to the owner of the restaurant, a stout little Chinese woman who had been fixing us with an inscrutable gaze. There was a rapid exchange of words and the woman came over to the table and told us politely that Peking Duck was their most expensive main dish and perhaps we would like to have a look at the menu before ordering.

'Peking Duck!' roared Hans again. 'I have money,' whereupon Otto gave a blast on his kazoo and the rest of us hastily shushed him, 'not now, Otto, not now!'

Otto, not to be silenced, gave another blast on his kazoo and there was a slight scuttle as Peter grabbed it from him and put it into his own pocket. Bobbish tittered, the Chinese woman stood there impassively and Peter asked to see the menu. Peking Duck was indeed extremely expensive, but Hans delved into his pocket to prove that money was not a problem and brought out an untidy bundle of notes which scattered to the floor. Getting down on hands and knees to gather them up, we could hear him counting under the table, and when he emerged, giving a broad and toothless grin to the proprietress, he ordered two Peking Ducks, two fried rice and two extra plates. They arrived and Hans divided the portions meticulously, bellowing to the waiter for more wine and beer. Peter thought that it would be a good idea to make sure we could pay for what we'd already had before ordering any more as the bill already came to 13,400 drachmas, so Hans pulled out his bundle of notes and proceeded to count them again, the Chinese woman standing stiffly by and watching him inscrutably. Oh, dear! He didn't have enough – there was only 8,300 there, mostly in 100 drachma notes. There was a confused pause while we all rummaged in our pockets and brought out what cash we had,

coming up with another 5,000 drachmas in notes and 470 drachmas in coins. Hans handed the money over with a regal flourish,
requested that his compliments be given to the chef, and we
marched out.

Soon after that my daughter, Kate, arrived in Patras and stayed in
the youth hostel for nearly a week. We had a lot of fun together
sitting in the garden chatting and drinking beer, and Peter had a
wonderful rapport with her. When she left to go back to England
we got ready to return to Italy. Unfortunately the motorbike had
ceased to function, and although Peter tried to fix it himself he was
unsuccessful and gave it to a wine house acquaintance. It had been
cheap, he told me blithely, it had served its purpose and he didn't
need it any more. End of problem.

An amiable and impoverished German called Andreas who had
been working in Greece, found the carefree attitude of Peter and Otto
so refreshing that he decided he would enjoy the vagabond life, and
asked Peter if he might accompany us on our trip to Italy as he
wanted to learn how we lived. Peter was agreeable as we both liked
him so, on Otto's recommendation, we decided to go via Igoumenitsa
and Corfu, where Otto had a girlfriend for us to look up. He assured
us that there were plenty of good towns for begging in on the way so,
early one November morning, we packed our rucksacks and left.

We went to Arta, where I stayed with the bags in the bus station
while Peter took Andreas round the shops to show him the ropes
with regard to begging – the only way of making money quickly
when travelling, he said. It wasn't something that he enjoyed
doing, Peter told me, but in the company of a friend it came easier.
They came back well pleased with the results and we took the bus
to Yoannina, in the mountains where it was bitterly cold and we
wanted only to thaw out in a cafeneion. We spent a chilly night on
a building site, and next morning the men went to work again and
after a simple lunch of souvlakis and beer, we went to Igoumenitsa.
It was slightly warmer on the coast, so as soon as the shops
opened the men went out with slightly more enthusiasm to beg the
money for the tickets to Corfu, and when they'd collected enough,
we boarded the ferry and arrived on the island a little after dark.

Otto's girlfriend was a prostitute who lived in a room in a derelict building overlooking the harbour, accessible only by climbing over piles of rubble and going through a hole in the wall. He'd given Peter detailed instructions on how to get there so we found it without difficulty. Dolly, the girl, was out but we left our rucksacks and walked into the centre of town, the men leaving me in a cafeneion while they went off to beg enough money for the evening and for breakfast the next morning. It turned cold and started to rain and they soon came back to the cafeneion, where we spent a cosy evening drinking beer and chatting with the locals. Dolly was still out when we climbed back through the hole in the wall, but she came in quietly during the early hours of the morning and was still asleep when we left.

The weather had cleared a bit, so after breakfast I went to the square to try and sell some watercolours, of which I had quite a good stock, arranging to meet Peter and Andreas in a little shop owned by a rotund old lady known as Mama Maria. A humorous character whom Peter had met on a previous visit to Corfu, she had a curious system of accounting, with old scraps of paper listing what had been sold in one plastic bag, and the cash she collected in several other plastic bags. She didn't trust cash registers and charged what she felt like at the time, depending on whether she liked the look of the customer or not. She had a strong dislike of gypsies and a suspicion of foreigners, she refused to sell to anyone who tried to haggle with her, and had the utmost contempt for foreign money, especially dollars, which she wouldn't accept under any circumstances. She loved Peter, though, and we sat in her shop drinking beer till Dolly came in.

Dolly was a good friend of Mama Maria, an attractive Jamaican girl, very black and cheerful, with a perfect figure and a wide, white grin. She'd heard all about Peter from Otto and told us how glad she was to have our company in the squat since she got lonely at times. We went back with her for a lunch of fresh bread and tins of ravioli from Mama Maria's stock, but no sooner had Peter started to heat it up on our little cooker, then we ran out of gas. Hungry and ever resourceful, he punched some holes in one of the empty cans, poured in the remaining kerosene from his fire-show kit and cooked the ravioli up on that. We all had a siesta, and in the evening Dolly and I went to a cafeneion while the men went reluctantly off to do some more begging. Andreas, initially so keen to learn how to survive on the street, found that he loathed begging and asked why we couldn't stay a bit longer and look for work. I explained that it wasn't easy to find jobs when one was travelling, particularly now that the tourist season had finished, and Andreas gloomily remarked that perhaps it would be better if he went to Holland, where he could work and where he had a girlfriend. Later on I told Peter what Andreas had said and he agreed with me that Andreas was not cut out for a vagabond life, but all the same he was 'a fine man'.

Peter had a simple way of categorizing people. Unless he was a 'fine man', which meant he was totally honest, friendly and charming, he was a 'fucker'. If he was an especially likeable rogue, he was a 'good fucker', but if he was particularly unpleasant and had no redeeming qualities whatsoever, then he was a 'bad fucker'. I think he considered himself and most of his friends to be good fuckers.

Peter wanted to give a fire-show while the weather remained clear, not only because he hated begging but because of the possibility of making considerably more money in one go. It was Saturday and he could only find pink paraffin for his act, leaving it outside Mama Maria's shop as the bottle was similar to her wine bottles and he didn't want her to get mixed up. As we chatted and laughed over our beers, Peter forgot all about it until we got back to the squat and when we got back to Mama Maria's in the evening, the paraffin had disappeared. The fire-show idea was cancelled and next day it started to rain in earnest, and our hopes of making money quickly were dashed. Peter tried selling my pictures in the shops but with little success, so he and Andreas unwillingly returned to begging for money. Damp and fed up, less than a week later they had made enough for our tickets to Italy.

5   A Not-So-Posh
Travelling Life

It was raining when we arrived in Brindisi and we caught the first
train to Lecce, Peter feeling that it would be a better town in which
to make money. He took us straight to Michele's wine house,
where we used to go when we were working for the circus, and we
spent a merry evening there out of the rain, Peter relaxed and
happy to be among old friends again. He found us a sleeping place
in the basement of a block of flats, and although we could find no
dry cardboard it was comparatively warm and draught-free. The
next morning it was raining as hard as ever so I went round the
shops to try to sell my pictures (without success), while Peter and
Andreas split up and went in different directions to do their
begging, hoping to make more money that way. Andreas had
finally made up his mind to go to Holland to seek out his girlfriend
and needed a large sum of money for his fare.

We spent another evening in the wine house and another night
in the basement, but after an unrewarding morning's collection for
both men we took the train to Maglie as Peter felt that smaller
towns were usually more lucrative. I went round the shops with him
to give him a bit of moral support and when we passed another
beggar sitting in the street with a sign in Italian saying 'I am hungry',
I couldn't help saying that it must be easier to beg like that without
having to actually ask for money. Peter didn't agree. He said that
begging was hard to do whatever method you used but that by
approaching people for money it was possible to make more in a
shorter time.

As Andreas didn't speak the language, Peter had written him a begging note in Italian on the back of a postcard, saying 'I am a foreigner. I don't have a job and I don't have money. I will be grateful for any help you can give me.' Peter preferred to speak for himself, openly and pleasantly, and his forthright manner brought good results because in most cases the shopkeeper would reach into his till and hand him a 1000 lire note. To his satisfaction we made rather more than expected and went to the wine house, where Andreas was waiting for us. It was still raining so Peter put off the chore of finding a sleeping place till later, and we had a convivial evening in the company of a portly little man with watery eyes and a strawberry nose. He invited us to stay in his apartment for the night, asking if one of us would be kind enough to cook for him and pointing out the large bag of groceries that he'd bought and which he was now too drunk to cook.

We all walked back to the apartment, delighted by this unexpected piece of good fortune, and while Peter did the cooking, Andreas and I chatted to the man, drank wine with him and looked at his family photographs. He was obviously lonely and I think he enjoyed our company every bit as much as we enjoyed the comfort of sleeping on a mattress on the floor, and it was especially luxurious to have the use of a bathroom and toilet. In the short time we'd been back in Italy, I was already having to become accustomed to the limited toilet facilities in the south.

The next day dawned bright and sunny, and before going to the station we took our host out for a few brandies, his favourite tipple. Then we took the train back to Lecce, as Andreas had decided to go to Brindisi to look for a lift to Holland with a lorry driver and Peter wanted to travel south. We said our goodbyes at the station and while Peter went to the market to beg, I found a place to spread out my pictures on the pavement. To my delight I sold a watercolour and two pieces of marble, and when I joined Peter in the wine house, I found that he, too, had had a successful morning and we had enough for the train tickets to Taranto with plenty left over. He told me that he wanted to take me to Siracusa in Sicily, where he knew of a cave in which we could stay for the wintertime.

There were a lot of other Germans living there and it would be a good place to spend Christmas.

I was hooked! The idea of spending Christmas in a cave in the land of the Mafia appealed to me, it sounded so very adventurous! I was impatient to be on my way, but we were enjoying Michele's wine and Peter, easily seduced, got inveigled into a card game with some friends and we missed the last train to Taranto, ending up in Ostuni instead. Peter found a sheltered spot to spend the night under a railway bridge and left me there with the rucksacks while he went in search of cardboard boxes. It was near the station so I suppose I shouldn't have been surprised at being awoken by the crowds of people passing on their way to work in the morning, all careful to avoid treading on us, but staring curiously as we emerged from our sleeping-bags. Not being used to the limelight in quite this way, I tried to look absolutely unconcerned as we packed up our rucksacks and tidied away the cardboard, as if it were the most normal thing in the world to be sleeping under a railway bridge.

Arriving in Taranto, Peter went round the shops to beg while I set out my watercolours and marbles on the pavement, but although a few people showed an interest, I sold nothing. We had a delicious lunch at the Mensa and spent the evening in a wine house near the fishing harbour, finding a secluded place to sleep between some huts on the seafront. Next morning we did a begging round of the shops together, and after a leisurely day we took the last train to Crotone, arriving at two in the morning and finding an empty goods wagon to sleep in. We went to a bar for breakfast and Peter chatted with the owner. There seemed to be an unusual amount of activity outside, people milling around, talking excitedly and frequently pointing to a spot on the pavement and Peter asked what all the excitement was about. The bar owner, looking far from happy, told us that three men had been shot down there the night before and he was a little anxious that the killers might think he saw too much and come back for him. I pondered on this as I sat with my pictures, thinking how swarthy and sinister the passers-by looked, but Peter merely laughed when I suggested moving on and told me that violent crime in Italy didn't involve people like us, and I was probably safer here than I would be in

England. In fact the people were just as charming and generous as Italians everywhere, and with Peter's help I sold five pictures and the last four pieces of marble, as well as being given a large plastic bag of food to take with us. It was again too windy to give a fire-show so we walked back to the station and took the next train to Reggio Calabria.

Despite what I'd heard about the high crime rate there, it was a town I liked immediately, old and sprawling with mountains behind, the sea in front and Sicily beckoning from across the water. There was a relaxed atmosphere, with people strolling in the road, reminding me rather of Greece, an impression reinforced by the sight of Signor Franco, who owned the bar where we had our breakfast and looked exactly like Mr Basil of the campsite in Kato Ahaia. We came across several other vagabonds there, including a rather sweet German friend of Peter's, and left our rucksacks in a back room with everyone else's, before going off on a tour of the town.

Peter took me first to a wine house owned by a friend of his, Don Paolo, a dear old man in his seventies with the face of an English aristocrat, fresh complexioned with snowy hair and twinkling blue eyes.

'Oh, Peter,' he cried as they hugged affectionately, 'it's so long since you were here! It's good to see you, boy! By the way, you haven't forgotten that you owe me 1000 lire from the last time, have you Peter?'

Peter chuckled as Don Paolo hurried off to get us some wine and told me that the old man always insisted that he was owed money. He was 'a fucker' but Peter loved him. We stayed there for most of the morning until it got too late to eat at the Mensa, so Peter took me to the market with him and we scrounged a plastic bag full of free vegetables and fresh bread, which we brought back to cook in Don Paolo's kitchen, stopping on the way to buy some chicken wings. Peter cooked a huge pot of rich stew which we shared with Nico, the quiet young German I'd met earlier in Franco's bar. When we'd finished, Don Paolo hurried over with an ingratiating smile, asking if he could keep what was left in the pot. As he took away the plates, Peter and Nico amusedly told me that he always did this when they cooked, as well as adding the leftovers on the plates to the pot, and reheating it all later to serve up to other customers. No opportunity to make extra money escaped him, so naturally he watered his wine too.

'But he looks so honest,' I said, amazed, causing Peter and Nico to collapse into further gales of mirth.

When Nico left us, we wandered to the park where Peter had a brief siesta in the warm November sunshine. Afterwards we went for an amble down the main street and were suddenly hailed from the other side of the road by a couple of buskers playing outside a supermarket, with their dogs. Peter hurried me across through the traffic, wreathed in smiles. After an exuberant welcome, I was introduced. The man with the guitar was Mario, hugely fat and jolly,

Mario

Wolle

with a mane of blonde hair and a beard, looking like a cross between Buddha and the Lion in the *Wizard of Oz*. His friend, Wolle, was tall, thin and black-bearded, wearing a black wide-brimmed hat that made him look like one of the early settlers of America. Mario was a noisy extrovert and had a bottle of brandy with him, insisting that we have a few swallows to keep out the cold. 'What cold?' Roars of laughter! Talking nineteen to the dozen, mostly in German but with the odd humorously succinct remark in English thrown in for my benefit, they exchanged the latest street gossip, who was where and with whom, good places to spend the winter and so on. Peter told them that we were making for Siracusa and Mario said that he might well join us there for Christmas.

'Then I might go to Ragousa for a few months. I've got a house there.'

Not wanting to sound too nosy, I said nothing, but I was surprised that Mario should be wealthy enough to own a house. I supposed that he lived the vagabond life for the fun of it. Over the years that followed I often heard people say 'I've got a house' and eventually realized that it wasn't that there were so many rich vagabonds – they merely meant that they *knew* of a house (shed, building, whatever . . .) and occupied it every time they visited that particular town.

At last we left Mario and Wolle to go back to their busking and continued our tour of the town. Later that evening we met yet another German who knew Peter from days gone by and went to a wine house with him, being joined by a couple of rather taciturn Italians, older men w;ith grey hair and flinty eyes, one of whom looked like Clark Gable, only more menacing. They invited us to share supper with them and ushered us into a little private room, where Clark Gable unwrapped a package containing a large salami and told us proudly that he had made it himself. He ordered olives, cheese and bread from the owner of the wine house, but there were no olives and the icy glare that the man received really had me worried. I felt so sorry for him as he hurried backwards and forwards, doing his best to please and fetching two different types of cheese, fresh bread and a large carafe of wine. I noticed that Peter's friend was talking to the men in the most subservient fashion, almost grovelling, and the atmosphere was not as relaxed as it might have been. I didn't understand all that was being said, but I wished that Peter would be more serious as his levity didn't seem to be appreciated. The salami was too fatty for my taste but rather than cause offence I stuffed myself with it, uttering murmurs of 'yum-yum' and 'buonissimo', which was a mistake as even more salami was piled onto my plate. After the second carafe of wine, Peter got out the kazoo that he'd confiscated from Otto, and gave an off-key rendering of a well-known Italian song. Frosty smiles stretched the faces of the two men opposite, but their eyes were as hard as pebbles. Peter looked uncertain but rather raffish with his tufty eyebrows and bushy beard and cautiously launching into another Italian song.

'No, Peter, not NOW!' I pleaded through clenched teeth and, beaming innocently at the men, explained that in Germany and England, when people have wined and dined in good company, they like to end up with a bit of music. Everyone laughed heartily but unconvincingly, and it was evident that Peter's music was not to their taste. The men must have realized that all serious conversation was at an end because it wasn't long before they got to their feet, shook hands politely and suggested that it was time for us all to go home. I think we were both relieved that the party was over and walked back to Franco's bar to collect our rucksacks, Peter playing the kazoo all the way, greatly to the amusement of passers-by.

The bar was closed so he took me to his old sleeping place in a disused building site, where there was cardboard already on the floor and some dusty blankets in a corner. It was a warm night and we had no trouble in getting to sleep, and next day the weather was like a good English summer as we strolled back to Franco's bar for breakfast. I felt scruffy and wanted to wash and change, but I couldn't see my rucksack anywhere, and when Peter described it to Franco, he looked at us in dismay and told us that a couple of Austrians with a car had taken it with them together with another pack. Franco had naturally assumed it was their property. I took the news surprisingly calmly, upset only by the loss of a dented silver locket holding curls of baby hair from my children, which was irreplaceable, but the only other things of real importance were my passport and address book which I had with me. The theft was inconvenient but it was a precipitate lesson in the folly of being too dependent on material possessions and my dejection soon passed.

We stayed a couple more days in Reggio, during which Peter gave a fire-show, but when the weather changed for the worse he decided that it was time to move on. There were several towns in Sicily that Peter wanted to go to, to make money before going to Siracusa so that he could relax for a few days when we got there. We took the ferry to Messina and travelled from there to Barcellona and Patti, where I was given fresh underwear, a lambswool pullover, tracksuit trousers and a pair of slightly too large boots to replace my plimsolls, which were rapidly disintegrating. All this time the weather was changeable and Peter was able to give only one fire-show, the rest of the time relying on making enough money by begging. Now that I no longer had my painting materials and pictures, I felt it was unfair of me to expect Peter to support me on his own, especially when I knew that he hated begging, so I asked him to write out a postcard as he'd done for Andreas, so that I could go 'shopping' on my own. Peter was very touched by my offer and wrote a begging card for me, but insisted that I use it only when I was in the mood and when I didn't want to do it, I need only say. Begging on my own certainly didn't come easily to me and generally I needed a glass of wine first to give me courage, but it was my choice to live the vagabond life so I felt that it was only fair to share the hard times with Peter as well as the good. We went to St Agata, then back along the route to Giarre-Riposto and Acireale, almost always sleeping in goods-wagons at the stations, Peter unerringly knowing which ones weren't in use so that we'd have a comfortable and undisturbed night. I think that he was secretly relieved to have some of the pressure of work taken off him and loved me all the more for my willingness to be a partner in all things.

Within a couple of hours of our arrival in Catania, we bumped into a German couple with whom Peter had travelled briefly a year or so before, and they enthusiastically invited us back to their squat, a house in a disused factory compound, well furnished and spacious. They collected water in canisters from the garage next door and used paraffin lamps or candles for light, and they shared their squat with five other Germans and Austrians as well as four dogs and two cats. Dieter and Fay, Peter's friends, had been there for nearly two years and their friend, Wolfgang, had lived there nearly as long, but the others came and went as the fancy took them. Everybody begged for a living, though it seemed to me that Fay and Wolfgang provided the most. Fay had a strong personality, but apparently not strong enough to coax her husband into action, because he hated begging and would find almost any excuse to stay

Catania Wolfgang

at home. He was a good-looking and interesting man and while the others went out to work, Dieter would prefer to sit in the squat and philosophize on life, with an admiring audience if he was lucky, with the cats and dogs if he wasn't. Although he was no older than Peter, Dieter regarded himself as the 'guru' of the squat and offered advice, in the most charming and persuasive way, to all and sundry – some of it sensible but a lot of it nonsense.

71

We stayed in Catania for over a week. Most mornings Peter and I went to the market to scrounge food for the squat and Peter usually did the cooking. Once he gave a fire-show in the town but was stopped by the police, fortunately after the collection had been made so we weren't deprived of our wine and cigarettes. In the evenings we all stayed at home, drinking wine, playing cards and talking, or singing lustily while Dieter played the guitar. There was a fat and elderly fisherman called Pippo, a Sicilian, who visited the squat regularly and he came in late one eveing while we were in the middle of an uproarious musical session. He clearly found this boring as most of the songs were in German, and after fidgeting for a while he said that he wanted to take us out for a cup of coffee. Dieter pointed out that at this hour the bars would all be closed but Pippo insisted that he knew of one just down the road which would still be open.

None of us really wanted to go as we'd been having such a good time, but Pippo was a friend and Dieter didn't like to refuse, persuading Peter and me to come along too. The bar 'just down the road' turned out to be a restaurant thirty kilometres away, not far from Augusta, and there was a wedding feast in progress with the guests all dressed up in their finery. However, our shabby apparel caused not the bat of an eyelid as a waiter showed us to a table where Pippo ordered steaks, garlic bread and beer all round.

'I thought you only wanted a coffee,' remarked Fay, a trifle testily.

'Well I'm hungry now, and I can't eat alone,' grunted Pippo. 'We'll have coffee afterwards.'

We did, after the steaks and another round of beer but, when the restaurant closed, Pippo was in the mood to continue drinking and took us to another late-night bar for more beer. Fay was getting crotchety. She was tired and wanted to go home, but Pippo told us that his fishing boat would be coming in soon and he wanted some fresh fish. Fay got very snappy but Pippo ignored her and drove us to a little bay where there was a shack inhabited by a fisherman friend of his who gave us wine and said that the boat was landing at a different bay that night. Off we went again and waited in a remote spot for what seemed like hours, Fay getting increasingly ill-tempered as the night wore on. The fishing boat finally chugged in at about four o'clock in the morning and Pippo went aboard, coming back with a bag of prawns for us and fish for the animals. At last he was ready to take us home, a magical drive with Sicilian music on the radio, a starry sky with a full moon above, the lights of Catania ahead and in the distance behind, the red-rimmed crater of Etna glowing in the dark.

Fay went straight to bed when Pippo dropped us off but the rest of us had started to feel perky again so Dieter cooked up the prawns and we ate them hot with mayonnaise. Everyone else was asleep except for the Austrian, Rene, who'd waited up to tell Dieter that three policemen had arrived just as we'd all left, in uniform and with their guns and, after helping themselves to the brandy, they'd had a session playing Dieter's guitar. They had wanted a soft drink to go with the brandy and as there was a large Coca-Cola bottle on the table they'd used that, and Rene had been too nervous to tell them that the bottle actually contained zibibbo, a strong and sweet fortified wine. He was rather anxious about the whole affair, but Dieter told him there was nothing to worry about as these police-men frequently called in for a drink and a chance to play the guitar.

By now it was early December and we had been in Catania for over a week but notwithstanding the fact that we were having so much fun in the squat, we weren't making more than enough to survive and Peter wanted to get to Siracusa in good time for the festival of Santa Lucia. He said that if he gave two fire-shows a night we'd not only have plenty of money for the Christmas festiv-ities, but that he'd have enough left over to buy trinkets from Naples to sell at the Patras carnival. I thought that it sounded a bril-liant idea, so a few days later, after a noisy evening in a wine house frequented by Pippo's fishermen friends, we said goodbye to every-body and caught the last train south.

6   The Cavemen

It was late at night when we arrived in Siracusa and everything was closed, so we slept in a little outhouse near the station and the following morning Peter took me round the town. After breakfast we went to a sunny wine house run by a Signor Russo, an agreeable man who reminded me rather of a clergyman. There were chairs against the wall and I was invited to sit while Peter stood at the bar and got into conversation with some Sicilians. It was all very cheerful and relaxed and in spite of my rumpled appearance the other customers, mostly older men, treated me with all the courtesy and deference so characteristic of the Italian people. I was eager to see the caves but Peter said that everybody would be out working at this time and we'd pay our visit in the evening. We left our packs and he took me to a different wine house tucked away in the maze of the cobbled streets in the attractive old part of the town. It was a lively, though dingy, little place run by a Mama Lopez and we had a cheap plate of pasta there before searching for some public gardens in which to have a much-needed siesta after drinking so much wine.

In the evening we went to yet another wine house, apparently known amongst the vagabond community as the 'Cornuto'. I didn't like it so much because there were no chairs and my legs were aching so we ambled back to Russo. At last Peter picked up our rucksacks, bought two litres of wine and announced that it was time for me to meet 'the peoples'.

I found it hard to believe that the cave could actually be in the town itself but, after toiling uphill past shops and through some blocks of flats, Peter shepherded me across a busy main road, we squeezed under a gate, stumbled along in the dark over rocks and thistles to where a rock face loomed up ahead and, all of a sudden, we were there. It was a vast cavern with a high roof like a cathedral, illuminated by candles and, round a table in the middle, sat a group of men playing a game of dice and listening to Sicilian music on an old radio. There were some dogs sprawled out on the ground and one of them bounded forward to jump up at Peter, wagging his stumpy tail and yipping with pleasure.

Bernd

'Hello, Goliath,' said Peter, fondling him, and there was a general cry of 'hey, Peter, you're back. Come on, sit down and have a drink.'

One by one I was introduced to the men. Sitting at the head of the table was Bernd, the 'grandfather of the grotte', a white-haired man with a neatly trimmed beard and a military bearing. Big Lupo was tall, thin and asthmatic, with a gentle manner and one or two words of English, while Little Lupo had masses of curly hair and big, blue eyes and chattered away to me in

Little Lupo

Eyetie Otto

76

Italian. Fresh-faced, white-haired Jurgen seemed to be a friend of Eyetie Otto, who looked a bit of a lounge lizard, but I took to Manny immediately. He put me in mind of a cuddly hamster as he shook my hand vigorously, beaming with affability and announcing in a voice that was rich with chuckles, 'I speak English very goodly and I talk properly Cockney. I was learned in the jail by my good friend Robert Morley. You know him? He is in the English BBC.'

Peter and I sat down on a sofa between Big Lupo and Manny and everybody started talking at once. It was all in German but I picked up the gist of the conversation and most of the time I talked to Manny, who told me that he wanted to practise his English and kept me laughing all evening. We played yahtzee and Manny explained that sometimes they played for money but if they were broke, as was the case this evening, they played for the household chores instead, the washing-up, fetching of water, chopping of wood and that sort of thing, which gave purpose to the game. When we'd run out of chores Jurgen took up his guitar and started playing to us, and very soon we were all joining in to sing the old campfire songs, German, English, Italian, and even in French when Peter started on the songs from his Legion days, until gradually people began to yawn and drift off to their beds. I slept on one sofa that night and Peter on the other, under an overhanging rock in the shape of a crocodile.

Manny

Jurgen

I was awoken next morning by a chorus of loud coughing and explosive farts, which reverberated round the walls of the cave as, one by one, the men arose from their beds. Manny brought me a cup of tea because, he told me, he knew how much the English liked their tea. Breakfast was a slightly quieter occasion than the previous evening had been, the men gazing silently into their mugs of coffee or beer, with merely the odd grunted request to pass the ashtray or the sugar. I was glad, not being at my best first thing in the morning. I looked around me and in the daylight I could see that the cave was well furnished, with beds at the far end and on ledges up at the back, Bernd's own bed being designed to look like a four-poster, complete with curtains and a pelmeted ceiling on which played a couple of cats. Against the cave walls and separating the living area from the kitchen, were cupboards and shelves full of books and ornaments, and, towards the entrance, a place for washing-up and another for washing and shaving. Just inside the cave a grate had been built for the wood fire on which the cooking was done, and later in the day Manny showed me a washing machine which they'd adapted to be worked manually, with a handle to turn the drum.

By mid-morning we'd all recovered from our comatose state and fell to discussing plans for the day, and not long afterwards everyone began to drift down into the town and the cave was emptied of people and dogs. As in Catania, the people all begged for a living, some outside supermarkets, some at traffic lights, each man having his regular spot. Peter and I had used up nearly all our money so we made a round of the shops together before meeting Little Lupo in the Cornuto wine house. We chatted companionably together in a mixture of German and Italian, Lupo easy to tease and ready to laugh at anything. He told us that usually everyone in the cave took it in turn to do the cooking and they all paid their share of the cost. Today Manny was making goulash, and tomorrow it was his own turn and he'd be cooking fried fish.

Everyone was back in the cave by lunchtime, loaded with beer, wine and food for the animals, some having made enough money to last for two days, others only enough till the next morning. Manny's goulash was first class, and he told me that he'd learned to cook when he'd been in jail. As we were all relaxing peacefully after the meal, there was a sudden puffing and blowing and stamping of feet, and a huge dog galloped in with a bearded man hanging on to the end of its lead. Dressed in a colourful anorak, with a bobble hat and a scarf in matching knit, he looked like an Alpine wanderer, and sat down with a crash and a shout of laughter, knocking over the litter bin as he did so.

'Oh, hello Carlo,' said Bernd unenthusiastically as the dog started tugging at the lead and barking frantically at the cats.

'Silence, Strollz! Donner wetter!' bellowed Carlo. 'I made 57,000 lire at the traffic lights today,' and he rubbed his hands together gleefully. 'Huh, I've already got 150,000 lire saved for Christmas. What, nobody playing yahtzee? Come on, let's have a game. I'm feeling lucky, ha, ha, ha.'

Carlo

79

Bernd, Peter and Big Lupo wanted a siesta, but the rest of us played, Carlo uttering shouts of frustration or triumph interspersed with loud laughter as he hurled the dice onto the board. We were playing for one hundred lire a game although Carlo unsuccessfully tried to raise the stakes to five hundred lire. I heard later that he always made more money than anyone else, I think because he was the only person I ever met, with the possible exception of Otto, who really didn't mind begging. He left us finally, in as much of a flurry as he'd entered, Strollz dragging him off at top speed, barking wildly with Carlo clinging to the other end of the lead, shouting threats and curses mingled with shouts of laughter. He lived in his own cave at the other end of Siracusa but visited the big cave regularly for a game of yahtzee and a chance to talk in his own language.

The next day, Mario and Wolle turned up, which meant there were now five dogs living in the cave, and yet there was never a hint of trouble between them. Of all the street dogs I'd met, only Strollz was badly behaved and we put it down to the fact that he was always kept on a lead whereas all the other dogs, invariably well mannered and obedient, were free. Occasionally Strollz managed to slip his lead and only a few days later, having escaped from Carlo, he entered the cave like a whirlwind, galloping round, chasing the cats, gobbling up what remained in the animals' food bowls, grabbing a pork chop that Peter was just about to put on the grill and bounding off with it before he could be stopped, and then lurking around out of reach and grinning until Carlo arrived to collect him.

With Mario and Wolle in the cave it was an excuse for another party and more singing, with Mario and Jurgen playing their guitars and Peter accompanying them on his kazoo. How the cave echoed with songs and laughter that evening, and how soundly we all slept afterwards, so that only Mario, Wolle and I were aware of the violent rumbling and shaking that signified an earthquake, they jumping up in alarm and I merely turning over to go back to sleep, hoping that the crocodile-shaped rock wouldn't fall down on top of us. Being accustomed to the frequent earth tremors in Greece, I wasn't alarmed, especially as I reasoned that it would be safer in the cave than if we were in a building, but to Mario and Wolle it was a new experience which they described in extravagant detail over breakfast next morning, enlivening the customary breakfast hush.

It was the 13th of December, the first day of the festival of Santa Lucia, and Peter was going to give a fire-show. We walked into town by way of the Santa Lucia church and saw, to our surprise, that all the stalls that had been erected the previous day were being dismantled. Peter asked what was going on and was told, to his dismay, that the big procession had been cancelled due to the earthquake. It was feared that another quake might follow, causing panic and chaos, so the silver statue of the saint would remain up at the Dome for the duration of the festival. In Russo's wine house Peter brooded over his beer, determined to find somewhere to give his fire-show as we needed the money.

So, late that evening and carrying the tools of the trade, we trudged up to the cathedral in the old town and found that the square outside was packed with people who'd come from miles around to see the statue of Santa Lucia. His optimism restored, Peter went ahead with his fire-show but, just as I was starting the collection, two policemen pushed their way through the crowd and called out to Peter to stop. I continued going round to collect what I could, hearing the men admonish Peter on his lack of common sense. Wasn't he aware that there'd been an earthquake and that any further tremors might result in wholescale panic, and that the additional danger of fire would cause a major catastrophe? Now, be a good lad and go home! They were very pleasant and sounded amused more than anything else, but even though we'd made a good collection, Peter felt frustrated. He didn't want to resort to begging and his plans necessitated a lot of money.

Next morning as we wandered into the town, Peter suddenly spied a Father Christmas costume in a shop window and perked up. *That* was what he needed to make money, he said, and went in the shop to enquire about the price. It wasn't too expensive so he bought it, and as we still had a little money left over from the previous night's collection, he bought a triangle and a tambourine painted with a colourful Sicilian motif. To my consternation we now had only a few thousand lire left, but Peter airily assured me that if he went to another part of the old town he would be able to give a fire-show without being bothered by the police.

We returned to the old town that evening in company with Little Lupo, passing the crowds of people outside the Dome and stopping eventually in another little square surrounded by pub-style bars and crowded with young people, where Peter put on his display. He was right. Although we didn't make nearly as much money as the night before, there were no police around to bother us. Lupo was enthralled by the fire-show and described it vividly when we got back to the cave, persuading Peter to give a short demonstration for everybody else's benefit. Manny was so entranced by it all that he asked Peter to teach him how to do it and the lesson commenced. To begin with all went smoothly and Manny managed to extinguish a lighted match in his mouth, to cheers and clapping from the rest of us. He extinguished another match and turned to us with his chubby hamster face glowing with pride. Next came the cotton wool ball and he put that out as well, to another burst of applause. Big Lupo nudged me.

'Isn't his beard on fire?'

Oh dear, so it was! As we all shouted warnings to him he turned to us again, beaming happily and oblivious to the danger. Convulsed with hilarity, we shouted all the more, waving and pointing until fortunately Peter saw the smouldering beard and quickly wrapped a coat over Manny's head. That was quite enough for the first lesson, Peter decided, and put away his gear but Manny was pleased with himself and told me proudly, 'You see me? When I liken to I am a fastly learner.'

Some days later we were joined by two merry young Austrians, Andy and Pauly, brothers who had been on the road with Bernd a few years before and who were among the founder members of the cave. They had always kept in touch with Bernd, who thought the world of them, and although they now worked normally in Austria, they came back each year for a visit to the cave. It was as if there was a breath of fresh air with them around, they were so youthful and light-hearted, ready to help and join in with everything. There were now twelve of us living in the cave plus all the animals. Peter and I had been allocated a double bed, which was perched on an uneven shelf of rock above ground level and which we shared with Goliath, the lovable little black dog who belonged to nobody and looked something like an old teddy bear. He was the cleverest of all the dogs, the king of the beggars, and there wasn't a garbage container in Siracusa that escaped his notice. He usually turned his nose up at the dog meat that the people fetched from the butcher, preferring to go off on his own (and adopting a limp for the purpose) to search for more tasty fare. He would linger outside a butcher's or baker's shop with a paw pathetically raised and he would invariably come away with some titbit.

Five days before Christmas, Peter decided that it was time to try out his Father Christmas costume. The plan was to go into all the shops and bars, Peter playing 'Jingle Bells' on his kazoo and beating in time with his triangle, while I went around with the tambourine and collected the money. In practice it wasn't quite so simple as Peter's lack of teeth made it more difficult for him to keep the kazoo clenched firmly in his mouth while he used both hands to play the triangle. Another problem was that Father Christmas needed a brandy in each of the bars we entered – to get a bit of the Christmas spirit – and as the morning or evening progressed, his beard would tend to hang awry and he would be bent double trying to guide the kazoo into his mouth. He also had problems remembering the tune after a while and would burst into the appropriate strains of 'What Shall We Do With The Drunken Sailor', one of his favourite ditties. When we encountered a group of gypsies who swarmed round us, plucking and grabbing at the tambourine, Father Christmas was not as benign as he might have been, swearing profusely in Italian, hitting the odd gypsy over the head with his merry triangle and kicking out at another with his merry black boot. But he was a novelty and the people loved him, and wherever we went he caused cries of delight from the smaller children and usually gales of laughter from everyone else, the lira notes piling up in the most satisfactory manner. I persuaded Peter to pay the money into a bank account so that he wouldn't be tempted to spend it all as was his wont, since he was still determined to save enough money to go to Naples to buy trinkets for the Patras carnival as well as having a good festive season.

Everybody in the cave contributed towards food and drink for the holiday and by Christmas Eve it was well stocked with beers, wines and spirits and an assortment of extravagant delicacies for the traditional 'Heiligen Abend' meal, which lasted until well into the night. On Christmas morning, after the unavoidable coughing and breaking of wind had died down and people were sitting round the table and grunting 'Merry Christmas' at each other, Andy played a cassette of German carols and made a large saucepanful of gluwein (like mulled wine) to put us all in the right mood. Manny and Big Lupo did the cooking for the Christmas dinner – fresh tuna baked in foil, rabbit in a wine sauce with creamed potatoes and salad, and even a pudding. Carlo came round for a game of yahtzee, staying on well into the evening until it became too rowdy for him, with everyone talking and shouting at once so that his own voice couldn't be heard above the rest, at which point he allowed Strollz to drag him away at the gallop.

Carlo was a teetotaller, one of the very few that I ever met on the road. Nearly all were drinkers to some degree, I'm sure partly because of needing the boost of alcohol to make the job of begging more tolerable, and most of the people I met were self-confessed alcoholics, but all the time I lived among them, I very rarely saw anyone drunk and incapable. On one occasion Manny wobbled rather unsteadily outside to pee, fell over backwards into the cactus and, unable to get up on his own, had to howl for assistance and was helped back into the cave by Little Lupo and Peter, both of them almost doubled up with unsympathetic laughter as, I have to say, were the rest of us. Perhaps it was the plethora of such hazards that prompted people to go to bed before they reached that wobbly stage.

We celebrated New Year's Eve with another long party; pot-roasted turkey for lunch and a variety of cold meats, cheeses and piquant olives to pick at during the evening, with masses of sparkling wine with which to toast the New Year. We sat inside playing yahtzee and listening to the radio until midnight, and then we all poured out of the cave as we heard the churchbells ringing out over Siracusa and watched the fireworks exploding into the night sky. A full moon with a double halo shone down on us, and I felt that I must be the luckiest woman imaginable as I stood there under the starry sky with Peter holding me close and telling me how much he loved me. We rounded off the evening with another singsong and in that candlelit cave, surrounded by friends, animals and with the man I loved, I don't believe that anyone, anywhere, could have been as happy as I was.

Mario and Wolle left soon after that but Peter and I stayed in the cave until the middle of January, when he suggested that we make a Sicilian tour while the weather was still good. He said that he'd take me to Corleone, Godfather country, stopping en route at various towns where we could make more money for our Naples trip. I was thrilled at the idea of seeing Corleone; it sounded so very romantic and exacting and it would be lovely to see a bit more of the Sicilian countryside. We went to Modica first, a lovely little place in the mountains, and from there we went to Gola, Port Empedocle and Agricento, staying briefly in each town so that Peter could give a fire-show. It was fun being on the move again and sleeping in empty goods-wagons or wherever we could find a secluded corner, and it made a nice change to be on my own with Peter. Most of the time I enjoyed sleeping out because it appealed to my parsimonious nature. But after some days it started to rain, the temperature dropped and Peter said there was no point in continuing as the bad weather looked set in for the winter.

So we went back to Siracusa and were greeted like long-lost travellers returning. Eyetie Otto had left the cave after a row with Bernd, who had discovered that he had debts all over town and accused him of giving the cavemen a bad name, and a German-speaking Sicilian, Salvatore, had moved in. Naturally our return called for another party, a raucous singsong ending up with Jurgen playing rock 'n' roll on his guitar and dancing energetically with Peter, who was playing the tambourine on Little Lupo's head, while their shadows flickered outlandishly on the cave walls.

We stayed there for another week until Peter decided that it was time to go to Naples to buy the goods to take back to Patras, for the carnival. We'd saved up nearly 500,000 lire, enough to buy five hundred flashing-light yo-yos and a hundred large balloons as well as paying for our fares all the way. Peter had sold the yo-yos that he'd bought previously for 1000 drachmas each, making a huge profit on the transaction, and as he'd taken orders for several more, it looked as if we had hit on an infallible product for making a lot of money. If we could have carried more yo-yos, we would have done.

From Naples we took the night train to Bari, Peter ensuring that we had a compartment to ourselves by taking off his shoes and spreading out our picnic of bread, sardines and garlic, and taking overt swigs of beer when anyone paused at our door. We weren't interrupted and slept undisturbed until the train stopped at Bari, where it felt excruciatingly cold after the mild weather we'd experienced in Siracusa. After the habitual round of bars and wine houses to greet his friends, Peter gave a fire-show to boost our already dwindling finances and that night we slept in the same church alcove as before. I was glad to get onto the centrally heated ferry to Greece the following evening.

7 Yo-yos and Eggs

When we arrived in Patras there was a minor hitch when a customs officer decided that we should pay duty on our yo-yos, but when his friend recognized Peter from a cafeneion they both frequented, it was agreed that three yo-yos each in lieu of cash was acceptable. Thankful that we had got off so lightly (though it hadn't occurred to either of us that we might have to pay duty), we took a taxi to the youth hostel, where Theodoro treated us each to a beer and told us that Otto had been banned from the youth hostel for bringing back a group of undesirables for a New Year's Eve party and, when a fight had broken out, had sat there giggling and leaving Theodoro to separate the men and to clear up the mess afterwards. Otto always caused problems, Theodoro added.

We decided to start selling the yo-yos straight away although the carnival hadn't started properly yet. We used to frequent a wine house run by another little old lady known as Mama Maria, a place full of cats and where Peter had sold his yo-yos for 1000 drachmas the previous year. Several other customers had also placed orders for yo-yos, so we stopped off for a drink there on the way into the town centre that evening. However, there is a vast difference between the time that an order is placed in the heat of the moment, when the buyer is flushed with wine and the zeal for a new toy, and the time when the goods have to be paid for. The first months of the year, moreover, are usually when people are suffering from the effects of overspending at Christmas, so when Peter entered the wine house, greeting everyone cheerfully and brandishing his yo-yos, the response was as might have been expected had we thought about it – the upward jerk of the head, meaning 'no' in Greek. I often noticed that in both Greece and Sicily, conversations could be carried on in complete silence, solely with the hands and facial movements. Perhaps this is to compensate for a normal conversation, which tends to be carried out at full volume. Anyway, for Peter the first refusals weren't too much of a problem, especially as we had glass after glass of wine bought for us to show that there was nothing personal involved, but later in the evening business was little better. Thanks to the novelty of the flashing lights, Peter did manage to sell two yo-yos to a couple of prostitutes who always drank in one of his usual haunts, but that wasn't enough to live on and he decided to cut our prices till the carnival started.

So we did, and business was a bit brisker, but although we managed to pay our way and live reasonably well, we weren't putting any money aside and I wanted to save the fare to England. So we changed our tactics and, instead of going round together, Peter covered the bars and cafeneions to make our living expenses, and I went round the shops to concentrate on our travel money. Even though I never went home empty-handed, Peter always sold far more than me because of his continual clowning, blowing his kazoo and that sort of thing. I had no sales technique.

On the first day of the carnival proper, the streets were crowded and we went into town full of confidence, certain that at last we could start making the enormous profit that we'd hoped for. But it wasn't to be. Peter started off by asking his original price of 1000 drachmas and within an hour he had decided to halve the amount, after which business wasn't too bad. We spent a further three desultory days in Patras with little profit to show for our efforts, and then we decided to try our luck in Athens. I had to go there in any case to get a coach to England and Peter had a yearning to visit a particular truck-drivers' bar where he could get good, cheap German food, served hot. He wasn't keen on Greek food, which he found too oily for his taste and which was nearly always served lukewarm or even cold. I didn't mind, never having been partial to 'piping hot' food which always burnt my tongue.

We arrived in Athens while it was still dark and found a cafeneion to sit in and drink beer until the city came to life, and then we went to Omonia metro station to see if we could sell any yo-yos there. It was the early morning rush hour, admittedly, but in less than two hours we'd sold double the number of yo-yos that we generally sold in Patras, and took a bus to Keratsini to the truck-drivers' bar, Peter's Truck Shop. There we tucked into massive plates of fried potatoes, onions, bacon, eggs and cheese, washed down with draught beer and all very cheap, and I understood why Peter had been so keen to have a meal there. There were a lot of Germans in the bar, including a very attractive woman trucker and two very much plainer prostitutes, and we passed a lively couple of hours there. We spent the evening going round the bars in Keratsini and selling more yo-yos, and then we went back to Piraeus where Peter had found a cheap hotel.

We stayed in Athens for three more days until I had my fare to England, where Peter said he'd meet me after 'making a turn' on his own. He told me that it was no offence to me but every now and again he needed to make a whistle-stop tour either by himself or in exclusively male company. I didn't mind at all as I, too, liked to do as I pleased independently sometimes.

My mother had bought me new painting materials and I worked feverishly to build up a set of pictures to sell. I also made some dainty caskets out of hen's eggs, which I cut in half, hinged, lined with silk, painted with a portrait or little landscape, varnished and decorated with beads. If not quite Faberge, they looked exceedingly pretty and I was convinced that I could sell them for a lot of money. True to his word, Peter arrived three weeks later and briefly met my family before we embarked on our travels again. Somehow he managed to lose his German Identity Card while he was in England, but he reported his loss to the police and was given an official-looking form in lieu, which got us through to France without a hitch.

The weather in Paris was terrible, raining so heavily that there was nowhere dry for me to sell my pictures, and it was an expensive city for us to linger in. We had enough money to get as far as Troyes, where it was still raining, and as we wandered around looking for a cheap bar to leave our rucksacks while we went begging, we came across a German sitting outside a supermarket, and after chatting to Peter for a few minutes, he invited us to spend the night with him. That was a piece of good fortune, so we made a cursory round of the shops to beg enough money to tide us over, and met Rocky, as he was called, in a bar where he introduced us to his friends, Herman and Daniel. I went shopping with the plump and garrulous Herman and when we'd bought all the groceries we needed, the five of us went back to their squat, a most beautiful place in one of a group of deserted farm buildings, with several rooms, electric light and television, and a cobbled yard outside with a water tap and surrounded by shrubs and creepers. With the exception of the cave it was by far the most attractive squat I'd seen so far, and the men kept it spotlessly clean inside.

Next day Peter, being a better salesman than I, walked round the shops with my watercolours while I wandered around delighting in the beauty of Troyes and looking for ideas for sketches. After a good, free lunch in the municipal canteen, I came across Herman, happily inebriated and in want of a bit of company as he looked for a present for his girlfriend. Of all the romantic gifts that he could have chosen, he settled on an expensive metal ashtray on a stand. After arranging to meet Peter and Rocky later in the railway station bar, I went off on the bus with Herman to meet his girlfriend, who lived several kilometres outside the town on an unattractive housing estate. As Herman spoke to me exclusively in French, I was beginning to get the gist of the language again. I always had a problem when I went to a different country because, although I could understand what was being said, I invariably wanted to reply in whatever foreign language I'd been speaking most recently. Peter was different, he could chop and change languages at will, without any difficulty whatsoever. Herman's girlfriend was a rather dour Frenchwoman, quite the opposite to his ebullient self, and although she was clearly unenthusiastic over the ashtray she gave us each a beer and we talked for a while. When Herman decided to take us both out for a meal, I felt that it was time to leave and went back to the station to meet Peter and Rocky and to have a few beers with them before going home to the squat.

We left Troyes early the following morning and hitched a lift to Langres, another pretty town where I sat with my pictures in the street while Peter went off to beg outside a supermarket. I sold nothing but Peter hadn't done too badly and we took a train to Beaune where Peter said he'd made a lot of money once before. Unfortunately it was a non-stopping train and we were swept past our station, ending up in Lyons late at night. There were no more trains till the morning so we were obliged to spend the night in the station, something that I would not recommend anyone else to do. The town of Lyons may well have been lovely, but we didn't stay to find out as the station certainly was not. It was uncomfortable and wherever we tried to stretch out to sleep, it wasn't long before we'd be disturbed by the cleaners or other station officials. I got hardly any sleep at all and was exceedingly disagreeable as a result, voicing my opinion of the station and the French in general in no uncertain terms. Poor Peter, he soothed me down, told me that he loved me and we took the first train out, to Tour-les-Pins, a pretty little town in the mountains where we had coffee and a good wash, after which I felt a lot better. We were running short of money again and, being Sunday, there were no shops open. We found a church and begged outside, and the people were charming and generous, also concerned because it was so cold and they advised us to take a train to Chamboury, where there was a municipal hostel. We did what was suggested and went to Chamboury, where we were given a good meal, beds for the night and the luxury of a hot shower, and the following day we took the train to Modane, on the Italian border. There was a slight delay when the police told Peter that he would have to say goodbye to me there since he had no identification on him apart from a paper written in English which meant nothing to them, but after a lot of jovial banter they let him through as well and we boarded the first train to Alissandria.

We didn't linger there but made our way to Reggio Emilia, where Peter said we'd be able to stay with some Sri Lankan friends who'd worked with him in Nando Orfei's circus. As it happened, they didn't live in the house any more, but the present occupants allowed us to doss down on the floor for the night. It was a good town for work and I sold three pictures before moving on to Forli, which Peter described as a beggar's goldmine. It was the week before Easter, when Italians are extra generous, and on arrival Peter went directly to a supermarket in the main street, where I left him sitting while I went in search of a good place to sell my pictures. I found a spot in a covered walkway and, with my pictures and eggs spread out in front of me, I sat down on my rucksack and commenced painting, not merely to appear artistic, but because I badly needed more pictures to enable me to capitalize on the time of year. Being early evening it wasn't easy as it was so cold and I kept having to blow on my fingers to keep the circulation going, but within two hours I'd sold four pictures and been plied with numerous cups of coffee or hot milk by passers-by, who'd say things like 'I hope you're not offended signora, but it'll warm you up.' As always the kindness and generosity of the Italian people never failed to amaze me. Feeling very pleased with myself, I went to join Peter and we found a perfect restaurant in which to spend the evening, the food being tasty and cheap, the wine good and the owners friendly and eager to chat. I thought I'd done well to sell four pictures, but Peter had made almost double the amount of money that I had just by begging, so we were both in very good heart.

We found a cosy sleeping place in a building that was being renovated, the only problem being that we had to rise extremely early in the morning to avoid the workers. However, there was a bar next door that also opened early, so we were able to take our time over breakfast and, because it had a washroom as well, I was able to clean myself fairly thoroughly every day. Although the north of Italy was more expensive than the south, the bars usually had chairs as a matter of course as well as spotlessly clean toilets that weren't 'out of order', perks that made our way of life very much more comfortable. We stayed in Forli for the whole of the Easter week. The delicacy of my egg caskets attracted a lot of attention, but they were expensive and it was my watercolours that sold. Demand for them was so great, in fact, that while Peter had a siesta in the public gardens every day, I had to sit on a bench and paint laboriously to replenish my stock – and yet however much money I made, Peter always made far more with his begging. We had never been so rich before. We always had our meals in a restaurant, we went to the cinema, we took a day off to go to Rimini where Peter had worked for several seasons in a discotheque, and we even spent a night in a hotel. The hotel was unscheduled, it has to be said, and came about only because we'd deposited our rucksacks in the left-luggage at the station when we went to Rimini, and the office was closed when we got back.

After work on Easter Saturday we left Forli and went to Rimini again as Peter had so many friends from the days when he'd worked there. We did the social rounds and went to sleep in one of the derelict buildings that Mussolini had had built for the poor people of Italy so that they could holiday in the resort of the rich – as we were doing. We spent most of Easter Sunday in Rimini and, to my immense satisfaction, Peter sold two of my egg caskets. I had hoped to make so much money out of my eggs, because of their daintiness and originality and the fact that they were handmade, but unfortunately they had taken me so long to create that I needed to charge a lot if the project was to be worthwhile and it appeared that few people were prepared to pay what I asked. Not only that, but the eggs didn't travel well in the rucksack and most of the caskets had developed slight cracks. Regrettably, it became clear that as a means to wealth the egg project was as unsuccessful as the yo-yo project had been.

We left Rimini and travelled down the spine of Italy, through beautiful countryside, to Faenza, Arezzo and then to Perugia, a lovely town at a distance from the station and at the top of a steep hill, up which we had to toil in the hot sun because there was a bus strike. Peter had hoped to give a fire-show in the beautiful old part of the town, but it was far too windy, and although he took my pictures and eggs round the shops, he didn't sell anything. He was further disgruntled by a noisy group of young beggars in hippy-style clothing, who were playing guitars, drinking wine, openly rolling joints and smoking them, and shouting to passers-by for money or tobacco. Peter said, scowling, that people who behaved like that gave all street people a bad name and anyway, he'd had enough of the north of Italy and wanted to go home now. So we walked back down to the station and took the overnight train to Reggio Calabria.

8   Deported!

It felt good to be back in the South again, and although it was still only mid-April, it was hot and sunny during the day and balmy at night. We stayed in Peter's old sleeping place, which was now occupied permanently by Nico and an emaciated little Frenchman with rotting teeth. Mario arrived in Reggio two days later in the company of a German called Zep, whom we never saw sober, and a pretty English girl, Sarah, who was almost as bad. The two of them, with Mario's two dogs and Sarah's puppy, all came to stay in the same squat, and a day later we were joined by two more large Germans, Michael and Holgar. It was very crowded, but companionably so, and Mario took it in turns with the Frenchman to produce culinary delights for everybody on a little camping-gas cooker. Peter and I always ate at the Mensa, where the food may have been inferior, but at least we had a bit of space and could eat in comfort.

At bedtime we all stretched out our flattened cardboard boxes, the silence of the night broken only by the contented snores and the morning heralded by the inevitable breaking of wind all round, with the exception of myself and Sarah. I came to the conclusion that women must be designed differently because it was the same in the cave – only I woke up silently. Peter told me that I snored, however.

Don Paolo's wine house had closed down, much to my dismay since I'd always thought him such a sweet old man, and Reggio didn't seem the same without him. We heard that the reason for the closure was that this same sweet old man had recently killed some-one and, solely due to his advanced age, he had been placed under house arrest instead of going to jail. Fortunately there were a lot of wine houses in Reggio so we had a good choice, but my favourite became one on the other side of the railway line from the station, accessible only by climbing through the railings or making a long detour by the road. It reminded me rather of the gypsy quarter in Patras, with its somewhat untidy surroundings where we could sit outside under a huge sprawling tree, drinking wine or ordering a meal from the kitchen should we be hungry. Mario was always hungry and I'd never met anyone else who could consume such vast quantities of food as he did, or drink so much either, and still remain standing. He was one of the people I liked best, a born-again Christian, always talking and laughing and without a trace of malice in him.

After two days of good living our funds started to run low again and Peter decided that I should learn the art of the Madonnaro, doing pictures, traditionally religious, on the pavement. I'd seen it done but didn't think that I'd be any good at working on the ground myself, not only because I'd never worked with chalks, but I didn't think that I could ever get the dimensions right on such a large scale.

'No problem, Baby-Prue, I learn you,' said Peter, dismissing my doubts with a careless wave of his hand. He bought a box of soft chalks in assorted bright colours as well as some sheets of stiff paper, as he told me that the pavements in Reggio weren't suitable for working on directly. Back at the squat, he showed me how to

rub the colours into the paper so that they'd stick firmly and how to mix the colours to get different effects of light and shade. I was surprised how capable he was but he told me that his difficulty was that he was useless at doing the initial drawing, which was the most important aspect of the work. I practised all that day, enjoying the challenge and finding it easier than I'd imagined, and by the following morning Peter felt that I was ready to go out onto the street and do it for money. With two fresh sheets of paper to work on, we went to the biggest supermarket in the main street and Peter taped one of the sheets onto the pavement outside. He wrote 'Grazie' ('Thank you') in bold letters by the side, and I got down on my knees to commence work on my first picture while Peter collected for me, rattling the tambourine merrily and calling for donations.

I did a portrait of Jesus in the morning and one of the Madonna in the evening, both from imagination and neither of them very good to my way of thinking, but we made just over 30,000 lire altogether and went to a wine house to celebrate. There we met an old man who told us how much he appreciated traditional art, especially that of the Madonnaro, and to prove it he bought both pictures for 10,000 lire each. From then on the worst of our financial problems vanished, since we had a source of income when we were on the road without the necessity for having to beg directly.

I got a great deal of pleasure in doing these pictures on the pavement and got progressively better as time went on. Sometimes Peter would get bored with collecting and would insist on helping me, but I guarded my work jealously, hating him touching anything except the background, which used to amuse him and provoke him into altering something very slightly and then drawing my attention to it, chuckling with amusement at my expression of panic as I checked to see that he hadn't ruined something vital. Often I worked on my own but I never made as much money as when Peter was there. We had a competition once to see who could make the biggest collection, working on opposite sides of the street, Michael collecting for Peter and Holgar for me, but even though Peter's picture was hardly started, and very much inferior to mine, he and Michael made a lot more money than we did, and I felt quite irked. Peter told me smugly that to make money on the street you had to put on a show – people were more interested in the artist than the art.

It was true. Peter worked with an air and a flourish, doing little except add a dab of colour here and there and sitting back with his head on one side to gaze critically at the effect, whereas I concentrated on my work, my head down and interested only in completing as perfect a picture as possible, but for him the money kept pouring in, while for me the appreciation was mostly verbal. My only advantage lay in being able to sell my picture afterwards, which was what usually happened.

Towards the end of April we felt that it was time to be making our way to Siracusa and we'd promised to be there for Bernd's fiftieth birthday. We took the ferry to Messina and went by train to Acireale, finding that their carnival had just begun, having been delayed because of the Gulf War. Not to waste this opportunity we bought some more paper and Peter found a place for me to work, staying by me to shoo away the gypsies that came swarming round with their hands outstretched. Never having worked amongst such vast crowds of people, I found it most unrelaxing with everybody milling about and having to contend with gypsy children trying to appropriate cash meant for me whenever Peter's back was turned. When the procession got under way, we gathered everything together and went gratefully to a wine house to spend a peaceful evening away from the masses. For the next two nights we slept on a building site, making plenty of money during the day and eating and drinking in the wine house every evening. Then we decided we'd had enough of the carnival and moved on to Catania to see Dieter and Fay, only to find that they were away and Wolfgang was looking after their animals.

We caught the last train to Siracusa, arriving at the cave very late at night. Only Little Lupo was still up, delighted to see us and have a chat. He told us that there were four people in the cave at the present, Bernd, Salvatore, himself and a German girl called Pamela, a strange female who never said much and whom I'd met in a wine house in Catania. Manny had gone to Rome, Andy and Pauly were working in Austria, Big Lupo was in hospital with TB and Jurgen and Eyetie Otto had gone to Augusta to work on a campsite, although they came back to help celebrate Bernd's birthday.

Big Lupo

By late spring the whole of the terrain in which the caves were situated was covered with wild flowers, the hillside a patchwork of colours – green and white and all shades of blue, pink, red and yellow. I was enthralled by the beauty and the variety, counting up to twenty-seven different wild flowers once, before losing count. We used to pick masses of them for the cave and stick them in jars, and I always picked a posy for Big Lupo when we visited him in hospital. Only Bernd went regularly, with the dogs, but usually one or two of us would accompany him, bringing with us fruit juice, toilet rolls or whatever else he needed. The hospital was an hour's walk from the cave, and after visiting Big Lupo one day, Little Lupo, Peter and I decided to pay a call on Carlo, whose cave was in the same direction but an extra hour's walk out of town.

Carlo's cave was very small and set into a steep hillside over-looking the railway line and the sea, and with a little tree in front almost hiding the entrance. To get to it we had to scramble down over the rocks, through thistles, grass and wild flowers and I could understand why he'd told us that a pair of shoes lasted him no more than six weeks. It must have been inhabited by the Ancient Greeks as there was a door cut square into the rock and several rectangular niches outside like those that had been cut into the walls of all the caves I'd seen, including the one we lived in. It was done up inside to look more like a caravan, with a wooden floor and a door, and walls lined with cardboard, with sliding panels behind which Carlo stored things, and an arched ceiling made with cardboard lined with aluminium foil. His bed took up one end of the cave and his kitchen the other, and in the middle there was a wooden table and a bench on which we sat to play yahtzee. With a little gas cooker and hurricane lamps for illumination it was very much cosier than our cave though I decided, when we got home, that ours was more aesthetically pleasing.

Peter suggested that we do a tour of Sicily and spend the summer in Sardinia, since without proper documents he didn't think he'd get into Greece. I loved the idea. We needed money for the journey, and in mid-May Peter and I went up to the Dome to make a large picture of Santa Lucia at a one-day festival to replace the one in December that had been cancelled. A few days later there was a festival in Noto, to which we went with Little Lupo, the two men taking it in turns to collect for me and sharing the proceeds afterwards. Then Little Lupo went off to Palermo to look up old friends and to have a bit of a change of scene, and Peter arranged to meet him there after we'd been to the festival in San Domenico in Augusta.

It was an auspicious beginning to our Sicilian tour because the festival proved to be particularly lucrative. When we got to Palermo, Peter located Lupo in the wine house as planned and the three of us took a bus out to Mondello, where Lupo and his friends spent most of their time. From the glowing descriptions we'd heard we expected to find a comfortable squat, but it transpired that they all slept on the beach under the pier and ate in a wine house in

Palermo or at one of the many beach bars. I wasn't drawn to Lupo's vagabond friends who seemed to be mostly German, but we had little time to socialize as Peter and I needed to get to work, since the fare to Sardinia wasn't as cheap as we'd anticipated and we had to start saving. The sleeping arrangements were far from ideal, especially since it rained in the night so we had to move to a more sheltered position under the pier, and then we were woken up again by Lupo arriving, full of beer and wanting to chat. Peter refused to sleep there another night and we found an empty beach-hut where we stayed till the weekend was over.

On Monday we decided to leave and, after saying goodbye to Lupo, we went to the German Embassy so that Peter could apply for a new identity card. He was told that since he had no other form of identification on him, he would have to go back to Germany, but he should be aware that he was on their computer and faced a jail sentence there. He was aware of that fact. The sentence was for non-payment of maintenance, and could be anything from three months to a year. We talked it over and Peter felt that our best plan was to spend the summer together in Sardinia as planned, and then I should go back to England while he went to Germany to serve his time and get new documents. He would also get himself a set of false teeth from the State.

That afternoon we took the train to Trapani, where Peter had worked when he first came to Sicily. He took me to a wine house for a drink, and later on we found a good place to work and stayed there until the shops closed. Just as we were packing up, an Italian beggar whom we'd met in the wine house earlier, wandered past and invited us to stay with him and his friend for a few days. We were only too pleased to be saved the necessity of having to search for a sleeping place, so we bought several bottles of wine and walked back to the squat, a derelict warehouse by the sea. The man's name was Patrizio and his friend was a lugubrious German called Enrico, who had a curious arrangement with his Sicilian wife, spending two days a week with her and the rest of the time in the squat.

After a rather disturbed night caused by lumps of plaster continually falling onto our bed, Peter and I went to work near the market

101

and came back to the squat at lunchtime loaded with meat and vegetables that we'd managed to scrounge, and while Peter cooked the meal, I chatted to Patrizio. He was a sweet, gentle man with a beautiful voice, originally from Milan, where he'd been a newspaper photographer. He told me, without a hint of self-pity, that drink and drugs had lost him his job, his family and everything he possessed, and now he was reduced to begging for his living. He said that he wasn't unhappy with the life he led now, because at least he was free from stress, but he admitted that he often got lonely. He was so interesting that I could have listened to him all day, but unfortunately it wasn't possible as Peter and I had to go back into town to make some more money, our morning's collection having been rather paltry.

We went back to the same place that we'd worked the previous evening and had only just started work when two policemen came and asked to see our papers. They were satisfied with Peter's typed form from the Metropolitan police, strangely enough, but as we had no residence permits we were invited to accompany them to the police station. There we were issued with deportation orders!

Thoroughly depressed, we walked back to the squat to impart our news to Patrizio, who seemed devastated to hear that we were leaving just as he'd got to know us. We bought some wine to enable us to drown our sorrows together and Peter started to feel more cheerful, pointing out that the only change to our original plan was that he'd have to spend the summer in jail instead of the winter, and another bonus was that we could use our deportation orders to take us out of Italy instead of having to buy tickets. We had been granted two weeks in which to leave the country, but first we needed to go back to Siracusa to pick up all my winter clothes that I'd left in the cave, and Peter wanted to tell Bernd what had happened.

Next morning we sadly said goodbye to Patrizio and his friend and took a train to Marsala, which Peter knew and where we did well with the pavement pictures before finding a wine house. We bought a roast chicken and more wine and he took me to his usual sleeping place in a derelict schoolhouse, where we settled down to eat, drink and be merry. Now that the decision to go back to Germany was out of his hands, Peter felt a lot happier, I less so because I wasn't looking forward to being parted from him for so long. The following day we moved on to Mazzara, where the streets were too narrow for me to work on the pavement and Peter left me with the rucksacks while he walked round the shops to sell some of my remaining watercolours. When he got back, footsore and weary after toiling all over town in the hot sun, we caught the bus to Agricento, where we slept in the backyard between some old houses, rising at dawn to get the first train to Siracusa, on which there was an incident that cheered us considerably.

At this juncture I must explain that although Peter never suffered from body odour or bad breath, he did tend to have a problem with his feet if he was wearing socks in the summertime, regardless of how frequently he washed or changed them. It didn't bother me as I simply adjusted my brain to dreaming about Greek salad with juicy chunks of feta cheese, but even I had to admit that on this particular morning, after so much walking about in the hot sun over the last couple of days, our compartment was not smelling of roses. Peter was asleep with his unshod feet on the seat opposite when the ticket collector came in, which caused the man to grimace horribly, utter some exclamations of disgust and wave his hand at the offending limbs, ordering Peter to remove them from the seat immediately. By accident his hand brushed a sock in passing and he turned pale, gave a strangled cry of horror and threw open the window to dangle his hands outside in the fresh air. That obviously didn't help as he fled to the toilet from where we heard the sound of running water and a lot of splashing. We were convulsed with laughter and didn't see him again.

When we arrived back in Siracusa we went up to the cave and decided to spend the weekend there rather than leave straight away. On Sunday there was to be an open-air Mass outside the Church of Santa Lucia, and Padre Rufino, who officiated there, asked us if we'd do a big picture of Santa Lucia on the flagstones in front of the podium. I'd never worked directly onto the ground before, but Peter assured me that it was no more difficult than working on paper, and he proved to be right, it was much easier than I expected. We had a lot of fun as all the young people from the church were helping too and there was quite a carnival atmosphere, the only real problems that we encountered being the frequent showers of rain that threatened to wash out everything, and the presence of Goliath, who was determined not to let us out of his sight now that Little Lupo was no longer in the cave. Poor Goliath, Bernd was too old and staid for him and neither Pamela or Salvatore paid him much attention so he was in for a dull summer.

It was now June and we left Siracusa the next morning, stopping off at Reggio Calabria to see anybody that happened to be there and having a last uproarious session in the wine house with Mario, Wolle and Nico, all of whom told us of the amount of times that they, too, had been issued with deportation orders. We took the night train to Bari, where we spent the morning drinking with all Peter's Italian friends, and after lunch in the Mensa, we started work on a huge picture directly on to the ground in the pedestrian precinct. It earned far more money than my normal pictures on paper did, so when we boarded the train to Forli that evening, we had a reasonable amount of money put by for when we needed it after leaving Italy, at which point we would no longer be able to travel on the strength of our deportation orders. Peter intended to get a travel warrant to Germany from his embassy in Milan, but as I had a valid passport I knew that the British embassy wouldn't be so generous and I would have to pay for my ticket to England. Peter also wanted to save some money to buy certain luxuries for his spell in jail.

On the train to Forli we had, for the first time, a slight problem when the ticket collector refused to accept our deportation orders in lieu of tickets and insisted that we leave the train at Foggia. Peter, enjoying the situation, refused to leave the train voluntarily and we were escorted off by armed police and marched to the station master's office, where we were ordered to pay for tickets to the Italian border. Peter refused and there was a lot of hysterical argument, Peter getting as excited as everybody else, waving his arms and asserting that he had no wish to leave Italy, it was only the

authorities that were forcing him to do so. Then all the station officials and the policemen started shouting at each other, and when I
interrupted timidly to ask if I could use the toilet, the station master
nearly had a fit.

'Why didn't you go on the train?' he screamed.

'I didn't want to then,' I said apologetically, 'I'm sorry.'

I was escorted to the toilet by an armed policeman, in case I ran
away I suppose, and when we got back it was decided that the only
thing to do was to put us on the next train going north and let
someone else worry about us.

We arrived in Forli the following morning and stayed there for
two days, working hard but not making quite as much money as
we had done at Easter. The weather was warm enough to allow us
to sleep outside in some gardens and, as always, we lived well,
eating in a restaurant every day and not stinting ourselves at all.
Before going to Milan we spent a day in Rimini, seeing all Peter's
friends and using up nearly all the money we'd made in Forli.
When we got to Milan next morning, I started work in the square
in front of the Dome while Peter went to the German embassy for
the travel warrant to his home town of Ulm. I was doing a picture
of Jesus, again from imagination and even more huge than the one
I'd done in Bari, and I was making a lot of money until a Green
Party group set up a publicity stall directly in front of my picture.
They told me that they wouldn't be long and gave me 10,000 lire
for any loss of income I might suffer, but as soon as they'd given
out all their leaflets, instead of packing up and leaving, as I'd
hoped, they got out bottles of champagne and had a jolly party
drinking to the success of their venture. When they noticed me
standing forlornly by my collection bowl, they gave me some
champagne as well, and when Peter arrived on the scene they
invited us both to join them in their celebrations and we were plied
with beaker after beaker of the stuff and weaved our way back to
the station in very much higher spirits than when we'd arrived.

Our last stop in Italy before going to the border, was Como, one
of the loveliest places I'd seen – an old town, very attractive,
surrounded by high mountains and with a lake stretching out in
front. Unfortunately it was also very expensive, but we made far

more money with my pavement pictures than we ever made in the South, and instead of spending it all in a bar, we bought food and drink in a supermarket and sat in the gardens to eat. It was unusual for Peter to forgo the pleasures of a bar when he had money in his pocket, but he told me that he wanted extra money for when he was in jail, apart from the consideration of my ticket to England. We slept in the station waiting room that night, and the following day we worked hard with the pictures before taking the train to Chiasso, on the border with Switzerland.

There we had to hand in our deportation orders which, for some reason, caused great hilarity among some young policemen who had to check us off the computer. They told us that we were free to take the next train back into Italy if we wanted and I tried to persuade Peter to do that but to no avail. He'd made up his mind to serve his jail sentence straight away, he wanted new documents and new teeth, and he wasn't going to change his plans.

So we spent the night in the waiting room and in the morning we caught a train to Zurich, a lovely town, clean, pretty and not exceptionally expensive. We set to work without delay, again doing a picture directly onto the pavement since those seemed to be very much more lucrative. Although we didn't expect to do as well as we did in Italy, to our surprise and gratification the money kept pouring in and by lunchtime we had already reached our target and went off for a cheap and delicious meal in the municipal canteen. When the shops closed in the evening we had made more than enough money for my ticket to England and Peter took me out on the town to celebrate. Naturally we had no desire to waste money on a hotel room and by the time it came to searching for a sleeping place it started to rain. Luckily Peter had noticed a suitable building site earlier in the day, although we found it locked up and he had to give me a leg up over a high gate to get me in, where, gorged with good food and beer, we slept peacefully until we were woken by the astonished workers in the morning.

We worked hard on our last day together and bought masses of coffee, sugar and tobacco for Peter to take into jail with him to ensure a more congenial internment. We went to the station for a few last beers together, I bought my rail ticket to London and, hugging tightly to each other as we said goodbye, we went to our respective platforms.

9   Travels with Otto

I was in England for three and a half tedious months, during which I tried every avenue open to me to find temporary work of some description, but without success. It was lovely to see my family and friends, but I felt impotent and restless and I was overjoyed when Peter telephoned me to say that he'd been released from jail. Just before leaving England I was lucky enough to receive a cheque for Income Supplement and as my mother refused to take any money from me, I went to Germany feeling like Father Christmas.

I was full of excitement at the thought of being with Peter again and, as the train drew in to the station, I caught sight of him on the platform, his eyes as blue as ever as they scanned the carriages. I felt that sudden thrill that always swept over me when I saw him and I almost fell off the train in my eagerness, a foolish grin on my face and almost lost for words.

We hugged each other hungrily and Peter took me to a bar near the station, where I was able to study him as we drank and talked, Peter full of schemes and new ideas for making money. I thought he looked a bit older and was definitely paler than when I'd last seen him, and he still had no teeth, but he was the Peter I loved, over-flowing with plans and humour and as irrepressible as ever. We took a bus out to Staig, where a jailmate had given him the use of his house. Peter showed me our bedroom and, going in to change, I gasped with shock as I suddenly caught sight of a naked leg poking out from under a pile of blankets and old curtains on the floor. Wondering, in mute horror, what Peter's friend was in jail for, I

109

forced myself to investigate and shakily lifted off some of the coverings. It was only a window dresser's dummy! We stayed in the house until Peter had collected his Social Security money and then we took the overnight train to Italy, stopping briefly in Munich for the Oktoberfest.

Having lived rather extravagantly in Germany, we needed to make money and get back into our normal way of life after more than three months of inactivity. Forli was our first stop and Peter went directly to his supermarket and sat down outside to beg while I went to the arcade with my watercolours, spreading them out in front of me as I sat on my rucksack and commenced painting. By the end of the day we were solvent again. We went to Rimini that evening and, after making the conventional social rounds to re-establish contact with everybody, we went in search of a sleeping place. There were gypsies in the building where we'd slept previously but it was such a warm night that Peter collected the obligatory cardboard boxes and we dossed down under a tree near the station. I felt incredibly happy to be sleeping out in the open again, breathing in the fresh air and looking up at a velvet, star-spangled sky.

We had breakfast and spent the rest of the day wandering round the town and dropping in every so often for a drink in one bar or another, eating in a cheap wine house and eventually taking the night train to Bari. Now that Peter had his ID card he wanted to spend a couple of months in Greece. We made the usual rounds of bars and wine houses where his friends gathered and one of the men, hearing that we intended to sleep down at the harbour, told us that he had a flat up for sale and not only were we welcome to use it, but it was unthinkable that we didn't. We were driven round to it at once and given the key, and for several days we lived there in comparative luxury, with a television, a fridge and a large electric cooker, on which we made our own meals instead of going to the Mensa.

Peter decided that as we had a proper address, however temporary, we might as well apply for residence permits, so we armed ourselves with passport photographs and went along to the appropriate office in the Civil Police building. We filled in the forms while we were there and handed them in to the bespectacled officer behind the desk. He scanned through them and his eyes lit up.

'Ah,' he said, speaking in excellent English, 'I see that you were born in Luck Ness. I was there once. I am very interested in the Luck Ness monster and I have many, many books on the subject. Tell me, have you ever seen the monster?'

I was just about to tell him that in fact I'd been born in Lucknow, India, when it struck me that I'd be wiser to agree with him.

'I haven't seen the monster yet I'm sorry to say,' I fluted, 'but I'd certainly like to. I always keep my eyes open in case she comes to the surface. Luck Ness is so very mysterious, don't you think?'

'Oh, I quite agree!' said the policeman fervently. 'I am going on another visit next year and have bought a very good camera since it is my earnest desire to take a photograph of – how do you call her? Ah, I remember! Nessie! Now then, my friends, come back tomorrow afternoon and I will have your residence permits processed for you.'

Peter and I could hardly believe our good luck in getting our residence permits dealt with so quickly and returned to the office next day, full of inner gratitude for my having the good sense to go along with the Loch Ness story. When we were shown into the office, instead of seeing a cheery smile on his face, our friend looked at us sorrowfully over the top of his spectacles.

'Why didn't you tell me you were deported from Italy earlier this year?' he asked sadly. 'Do you have permission to re-enter this country?'

'Well, no,' said Peter, puzzled. 'We were told that we'd been crossed off on the computer and were free to re-enter at any stage.'

'I'm afraid that is *not* the case. Before you returned you should have gone to the Italian embassy in your own country to obtain official clearance. Now, under normal circumstances I would have to give you fresh deportation orders but I like you both and we have an interest in common. Take these applications away with you and destroy them and let us pretend this conversation never took place. Goodbye, my friends!' He shook hands and ushered us out.

So we went back to our illegal status and hoped for the best. Arriving home after a session at the wine house one evening, we found two men waiting for us, or rather, waiting to take Peter out for a drink, the invitation being expressed in such a way that it certainly couldn't be refused. I was obviously not included so I went up to the flat and settled down to an evening of television. Many hours later Peter returned, extremely sober and keen that we should make the money for our ferry tickets to Greece without further delay. He said that he had been taken to what seemed like a private club, where he'd been wined, dined and offered a woman (!), and interrogated by men considerably older than himself, who had talked knowledgeably about politics and especially the politics of unstable countries. They had appeared to know a lot about his life and had questioned him closely on his knowledge of firearms and his political opinions, and he'd received the distinct impression that these people were looking for someone without too many scruples to use in some illegal operation. Not wanting to become involved, Peter told me that he had 'played the stupid man', the beggar who was interested only in making enough money for his next drink, and eventually his frivolous attitude had persuaded them to lose interest and he had been driven home.

I had been selling my watercolours surprisingly well in Bari and making quite enough money to live on, but the day after his encounter with the men, Peter wanted me to make a really big picture on the flagstones in the pedestrian precinct while he collected for me, so that we could make the money to leave Italy in one fell swoop. By the time the shops closed we had made more than either of us had anticipated and, to ensure that we would be comfortably off for a while, Peter gave a fire-show that evening. We collected our rucksacks and had a last drink with everybody who'd been so kind to us, said our goodbyes and, with a certain amount of relief, boarded the Patras-bound ferry.

As soon as we arrived in Patras we made our habitual round of the cafeneions and wine houses and by the time we reached the youth hostel we were both feeling very mellow. We found that Otto was back at the hostel, his ban having been lifted on a promise of good behaviour, and this time he was with a rather withdrawn young Austrian by the name of Wolfgang, who had a perpetual sniff and a limp. Otto was never with the same travelling companion for long, presumably because they all found him too noisy and overpowering for more than a few weeks. Peter and he were overjoyed to see each other after such a lapse of time, of course, and they spent the next few days almost exclusively in each other's company, Otto insisting that they went begging together as they always had such a good laugh. Then Otto suggested that we all go to Crete for the winter as he had a good friend living there who was a zealous member of the

Wolfgang

International Church and was bound to do his best to help us in any way he could, apart from which, averred Otto, the winter in Crete was warm and sunny. We would make the money for our tickets in all the little towns en route to Athens, stopping off at Diakopto for a few days on the way, staying in a deserted camp-site for a little holiday, lazing on the beach all day and cooking over a campfire at night.

It sounded most enticing and Otto's enthusiasm was so infectious that we all packed our rucksacks and checked out of the youth hostel, taking a train that evening for Aigio, a few stops along the line and, according to Otto, a good town for begging. It was late when we got there but we were already happily inebriated and fell asleep in the dry grass on the far side of the railway line. Next morning we left our rucksacks in the waiting room and went into the town for a lengthy breakfast. All the men had kazoos and went off busking, leaving me to go back to the station to wait for them. It wasn't long before Otto turned up to take me for a beer at the nearest port of call, which happened to be the local bordello. He got into conversation with a German-speaking prostitute and, knowing that I was keen to get a bit of practice doing quick portraits, suggested that I sketch the girl while they talked. It was an ideal opportunity for me and the girl was delighted with the portrait, calling over two of her colleagues so that I could sketch them as well. We had a most entertaining morning. The girls bought beer after beer for both of us, gossiping with Otto while I worked, and afterwards they gave me 500 drachmas for each portrait, which may not have been a fortune, but seemed a lot of money for doing very little and struck me as being a particularly pleasant way of making a living. After a while we were joined by Peter and Wolfgang and the four of us went back to the station to get a train to Diakopto.

We arrived at lunchtime and sat in a cafeneion drinking more beer until it was generally agreed that we should get ourselves organized for our stay on the campsite, whereupon we bought a joint of lamb, assorted vegetables and a crate of beer, and took a taxi out of town to where it was situated. The campsite was every bit as lovely as Otto had promised, full of trees and with mountains towering behind and the crystal-clear sea in front. There were little wooden huts in amongst the trees, with a fresh-water tap for our needs, and when we'd collected enough wood, Peter got a fire going and we made a rich soup in an old olive oil can that we found, fishing the lamb out at the end and grilling it over the embers. As darkness fell and the stars came out, so did the kazoos, and it was the sound of our merriment floating over the night air that attracted a group of four Albanians who told us that they, too, were staying on the campsite in one of the huts. We offered them beer and they sat down solemnly on some old plastic chairs that we'd found lying around, but they were humourless characters who seemed to look down on our way of life, casting rather a damper on the evening. When the beer ran out we made our excuses and laid out our sleeping bags for the night, and the four Albanians drifted away.

Next morning we walked back into town for our breakfast and Otto scrounged some potatoes which, after another long beer session in the cafeneion, we took back to the campsite along with a fresh crate of beer and a tub of tzatziki. The olive oil can was still half full of soup so Peter got the fire going again and we drank several mugfuls of that while we waited for the potatoes to bake in the embers. Satiated and sleepy, we all had a siesta in the warm October sunshine, building up the fire again when we awoke and eating the potatoes filled with tzatziki and washing it all down with more soup and beer. Then the men brought out their kazoos for another musical session and it wasn't long before we were joined by the four Albanians. Although polite enough, they lacked a sense of fun and we didn't enjoy their company. In the morning we all felt that it was time to move on so we packed our rucksacks and walked back into Diakopto to take the next train to Xilocastro.

Peter and Otto went off to go round the bars and cafeneions, while Wolfgang and I went round the restaurants to sell my pictures. We sold several and felt pleased with our evening's work, but when we met Peter and Otto later, they were not so happy. They'd been doing very well for the first half hour, but after that they'd been stopped by the police who accused them of being Albanians and wanted to see their work permits. They were cautioned and sent on their way, but work was effectively cancelled for the time being so they spent the rest of the evening in a cafeneion. Peter was tetchy and took me off with him to another cafeneion, where he told me he'd had enough of Otto's incessant chatter and wanted to spend a peaceful hour on his own with me. After a while he brightened up and we went back to the station and bedded down in an empty goods-wagon, and next day we moved on to Corinth. Leaving our rucksacks in the waiting room at the station, we walked into town to find a cheap restaurant where we ate a plate of cold chips and stuffed tomatoes, and afterwards we went in search of a cafeneion in which to settle down for an evening of beer and laughter. Peter's good humour had long since been restored. He told us that it was his aim to beg on an aeroplane, something that he was sure nobody else had done. Otto seized gleefully on the idea and they set about making plans and laughing like a couple of schoolboys.

Listening to them sniggering away, I had been sketching them idly, and the woman who ran the bar noticed what I was doing and asked me to sketch some friends of hers who were sitting at another table, and whatever it cost she would pay. I was more than happy to oblige and all of a sudden I was inundated with customers wanting portraits for 500 drachmas a time plus beers for the four of us. I had every bit as much fun as I'd had with the prostitutes and made a fat profit at the end of it, we'd all been drinking gratis, and as we left we were requested to come back the following day as there would be more work for me, so all in all it had been a good evening. Peter and I wandered off for a tranquil hour on our own again and by the time we got back to the station Otto and Wolfgang were already asleep under a tree.

Next morning we found the station crowded with Albanians so instead of breakfasting there we walked back to the bar of the previous night. After a few beers the men took their kazoos and went off to do a round of busking, leaving me to get on with some portraits and coming back for lunch to find me still at work. I did nothing else all day in fact and there seemed no end to the beers that were being sent to our table, until at last the bar closed and we made our buoyant way back to the station. There we discovered that my rucksack was missing! Being the second time that this had happened it came as no more than a dull shock because my sleeping-bag was in Peter's pack and I had my purse, my water-colours and my painting materials with me. When I realized next morning that once again I was left with only the clothes I was wear-ing and there were no church-run charities where I could be reclothed for nothing, I felt a bit irked but Peter was incensed. He had never before expected thieving in Greece, which was the one country that we had always been able to leave our belongings with-out fear of them disappearing, the Greeks having a well deserved reputation for honesty with personal property, and as he sat there fuming, his desire to continue to Crete evaporated. He wanted to go back to Sicily for the winter.

But now that Peter had decided not to continue the journey to Crete, Otto also lost his enthusiasm for the venture so, after one more day in our cafeneion, where I still had some portraits to do, the four of us took the train back to Patras and checked in at the youth hostel again. I had a bit of luck, because when Dana heard about the theft of my rucksack she offered me various items of clothing that had been discarded by other backpackers, so I had a welcome change of clothing to last until we got to Italy, after which I would have no more problems.

For several days the three men went out with their kazoos but inevitably they got sidetracked into cafeneions until eventually Peter, who was keen to leave Greece, decided he would do better to go round the restaurants with me and sell pictures. Naturally I was delighted with this arrangement since it meant that we spent more time together, and after work we always called in to Mama Maria's wine house for a peaceful glass of wine in the company of Peter's Greek friends. The only trouble was that it was now late in October, too late for the summer trade and too early for Christmas, and although we sold enough to pay our way, we never managed to save anything. We talked it over and came to the conclusion that if we checked out of the youth hostel and slept rough for a while, it shouldn't take too long before we saved the money to go to Italy.

Immediately Otto and Wolfgang did the same, accompanying us to Rio where Peter intended to 'make shiffs' which by now I realized meant begging on the ferry boats, and while they all went begging, I sat in a cafeneion and painted pictures until they'd made enough for the day, at which point they all returned to the cafeneion for refreshment. When it got dark we all took the ferry to Antirrio, on the other side, and found a cheap restaurant to spend the evening in, sleeping on a building site and going back to Rio next morning to work.

I sold two watercolours while I waited for the men, and when they came back at lunchtime, flush with money, the party commenced again, even more lively this time as we were joined by an extremely jolly little German, Franz, who ran a bakery in Rio. When he left we took the ferry to Antirrio for a filling meal of cold mince and spaghetti and in the evening Franz turned up with his family, the men settling down to play a noisy game of cards while Franz's wife, Irmgard, chatted to me in rapid German interspersed with gusts of laughter and their two little girls ran wild with a small, hairy dog. The party became so uproarious that eventually Franz announced he would take us back to their apartment for fried eggs and home-made bread. He bought a crate of beer and we all piled

117

into his small estate car to drive back to Rio, which would have been a nerve-racking experience had we been sober. Fortunately we weren't, and we all laughed hysterically as Franz drove erratically along the road, the car swaying from side to side, unused to its unusually heavy load, and swerving every now and again to avoid the oncoming traffic. On arrival at the apartment Irmgard, still talking nineteen to the dozen and laughing gustily, produced fresh bread and plate after plate of fried eggs, which we washed down with beer as we listened to cassettes of German music, accompanied by Peter, Otto and Wolfgang on their kazoos, the little girls meanwhile racing madly round the room with their dog and a cat. It got too late to go back to the building site so we all stayed the night and slept on the floor, and in the morning Franz drove us back to Rio.

We spent the next two days making enough to live on and spending it all in the cheap restaurant and the cafeneion, but it started to rain hard and we felt that it was time to go back to the youth hostel in Patras. Peter was beginning to hanker for Italy. He said that in Otto's company it was impossible to save money so he would go on a begging tour alone, leaving me at the youth hostel. It was the obvious solution, of course, and I didn't mind staying on my own at the youth hostel while Peter was away for a few days. However, the cunning plan was foiled when Otto decided that he and Wolfgang would go along as well to keep Peter company, and while Peter made the ticket money, he and Wolfgang would make the money to live. It sounded feasible but I had my doubts as to whether it would be as simple as all that, and I was right. Three days after leaving, Peter and Wolfgang arrived back in Patras, having got as far as Corinth, where Otto had met another German and had decided to abandon the plan to make money for tickets, and had wanted Peter to stay there and have a good long party instead. By this time Wolfgang, too, was tiring of Otto's company, so he had come back with Peter and wanted to come to Italy with us.

There were two duty-free shops in Patras, one at each end of the port, and it was fairly common practice for anyone with a ticket to stock up with duty-free goods prior to leaving, and go back into the town to sell them in certain bars and cafeneions at a small profit. Peter had done it himself on various occasions when his Greek friends, unwilling to run the risk themselves, had asked him to provide them with spirits and cigarettes, and now he offered his services once again. I didn't like the idea and said as much but Peter insisted that it was the only quick way to make the money to go to Italy.

His Greek friends and acquaintances, deprived of their duty-frees for so long, were delighted that he was back in business, and he was immediately given several large orders with payment in advance, and set off boldly to get the goods. I went with him the first time, slightly apprehensive because he had no ticket, and was amazed at how simple it was, nobody asking to see the tickets or even querying the amount of bottles we were buying, which was considerably more than the legal limit. After the first run, he was given a whole lot more orders and did the same thing at the other shop, and with the profit he had made, he had enough money to buy the ferry tickets. But business wasn't over as more Greeks wanted duty-free goods and tried to persuade Peter to make another sortie. I told him that he would be pushing his luck if he tried to do it a third time, but as I hadn't been to the shop at the far end of the port, I offered to go myself if Wolfgang came with me to help carry the goods.

Wolfgang agreed to do this, but bought his ferry ticket for the next day just to be on the safe side, and off we went to the duty-free shop and bought everything that was on the list. All went well and we were almost at our journey's end and walking through the dock gates with our plastic bags clanking away merrily, when we were apprehended by two port policemen. They demanded to know what we were doing with so many bottles of spirits and ciga-rettes and Wolfgang told them that we were merely taking them back to pack in our luggage before leaving the next day, producing his ticket as proof. The policemen clearly didn't believe him, and it did seem an unlikely story in view of the number of bottles we had, but Wolfgang stuck doggedly to his story while I sat there trying to appear innocent.

'But what is the problem?' I pleaded. 'We're not stealing, we have the receipt. Everything's been paid for.'

'The problem is that you're smuggling,' I was told firmly, at which I looked even more confused.

'But I don't understand. How can we smuggle goods into the country where we bought them? I thought it was only possible to smuggle goods into a foreign country.'

There was a pause while the two policemen looked at each other and wondered how to explain the law, and one of them admitted that it was indeed obscure and he accepted that it was simply a misunderstanding on our part, but the fact remained that we couldn't take our purchases out of the port unless we paid the duty on them. I asked if perhaps we could leave our goods in the port police office and collect them before we left the following evening and, to my great relief and effusive thanks, the policemen agreed that that would be the best solution.

Peter was waiting for us in the cafeneion, annoyed that we could have been so stupid as to get caught. To prove that he could succeed where we had failed, he marched out straight away and made two further trips for duty-free goods to recoup the money we had lost, and the following day we were able to check out of the youth hostel and buy our tickets for the ferry to Italy.

120

10 The Season of Goodwill

We retrieved our bags of duty-free spirits and cigarettes and had an unusually lively voyage drinking our own whisky, which had the effect of changing Wolfgang from his normal stolid and introverted self into an animated travelling companion. We arrived in Bari mid-afternoon and sat in a little park until the wine house opened, getting into conversation with an amiable Austrian by the name of Franco, also a vagabond, who slept on the rocks behind the harbour wall with his three dogs. He said he had plenty of beds and we were welcome to stay with him.

We accepted gratefully as he was such an easy-going character and it saved us the trouble of having to search for a sleeping place. He wasn't joking about the beds either, as there were five metal bedsteads lined up on that stretch of rocks, without mattresses but with perfectly good springs. Apart from an icy wind it was a nice spot, tucked away out of sight of the town and difficult to get to over the rocks, so there was little chance of being disturbed. There was plenty of driftwood lying around too, so we built a fire and Franco cooked us a meal, the four of us sharing a bottle of duty-free whisky to help insulate us against the cold.

Next morning, the weather being too windy to enable me to put my pictures out on the pavement to sell, I walked round the shops with them in the hope that I might find a buyer, but without success. Meanwhile Franco and Wolfgang went into town with the dogs and Peter, leaving the cigarettes and one bottle of whisky for Franco, took the rest of the duty-frees to the wine house to see if any of his black-market friends were interested in buying them off him. When

121

I met him later, he told me that although he'd got his money back, he'd made no profit at all, and after all the hassle we'd gone through, it was the last time he was going to get involved in the duty-free racket. Franco and Wolfgang arrived with the dogs and we all sat in the park drinking beer and eating pizza to keep us going until the evening. I had the beginnings of a cold, my nose wouldn't stop running and I longed to get back to the warmth of Sicily. Peter also wanted to be on the move again and as the next day was Sunday it was a good opportunity to make money outside the churches. Bari was too full of other beggars so he suggested that we try Gioia di Colle, a little town on which he had no information work-wise, only a basic gut feeling. We spent another draughty night on the rocks with Franco, and in the morning we took the first train there.

We must have looked a sorry trio as we walked into the town centre, Peter with his habitual rasping cough, Wolfgang limping along with his perpetual sniff, and myself bringing up the rear with blisters on both feet and constantly blowing my increasingly red nose. We left Wolfgang at the first church we came to and went further into town, coming to another church with a little square in front, perfect for doing a picture of the Madonna directly onto the paving stones. We made very much more money than we expected and, since Wolfgang was nowhere to be seen, shared a large plate of pasta and went in search of a wine house, finding a bar instead, where the people were so friendly that we almost felt as if we'd lived in the town all our lives. We met up with Wolfgang later and heard that he, too, had made far more money than was usual and afterwards he'd been taken out for a meal by one of the members of the congregation. Gioia di Colle was a town to remember!

That night we took the train to Reggio Calabria, waking up as the train chugged in, to the most glorious sunshine in which my cold vanished as if it had never existed. We had lunch in the Mensa and then went to the wine house on the far side of the railway lines, where we ran into Mario, Wolle, Nico and two other gregarious Germans, Thomas and Lutz. It was a wonderful, noisy reunion, everyone talking animatedly, laughing, joking and catching up with the latest gossip on the street. Peter and I spent the night with

Mario and Wolle in a shack near the beach, and Wolfgang limped off with Lutz. In the morning we all went into town together, and I bought some paper to start work on a new picture while Peter went off busking with Mario and Wolle, playing a raucous accompaniment to the guitar on his kazoo. That evening we took the ferry to Messina and caught the last train to Siracusa.

We reached the cave at midnight and marched in, Peter and Wolfgang playing 'Jingle Bells' in excruciating disharmony, guaranteed to wake even the heaviest sleeper. In fact nobody had gone to bed, although the atmosphere was far from lively, with Bernd, Salvatore and Eyetie Otto arranged glumly round the table at which sat an exceedingly dirty and drunken individual, who rose unsteadily to shake hands and leer at me, introducing himself as Gerhardt, a friend of Eyetie Otto. We discovered that Big Lupo was still in hospital, Jurgen continued to work on the campsite in Augusta, while Pamela had left Siracusa in the company of a passing Austrian, and there was an air of general despondency amongst those who remained.

Next morning we discovered that there was no longer any sort of order in the cave and the whole place seemed to have gone to rack and ruin. The table was filthy, piles of mouldy pots and crockery lay festering in the washing-up area, there was no water, and the little adjoining cave that served as the toilet was indescribable. It was obvious that people no longer bothered to do the simplest of chores, not even the cooking because it was too much of an effort to chop the wood and fetch the water. Peter, having given Wolfgang such an appealing description of our life in the cave, had some harsh things to say and we all got to work to clean everything up, he and Salvatore filling the water canisters and chopping wood, I doing the washing-up, Gerhardt, sober, wiping the table and sweeping the floor, while Bernd and Wolfgang incinerated the horrors in the toilet cave. Eyetie Otto slipped away before his services could be called upon and he didn't come back, but that evening two Sicilians turned up at the cave to find out where he'd gone as he owed them money and they wanted payment. Life went back to normal and in the next few days Manny arrived, just as sweet as ever, and shortly afterwards Little Lupo returned after a

123

spell in hospital in Palermo, so we had a good excuse to celebrate and it was almost like old times. Some days later Salvatore brought home a Spaniard whom he'd met in Russo's wine house, Antonio by name and an ex-Legionnaire turned vagabond (like Peter), who fitted well into our way of life.

Manny had spent several months in a clinic in Austria, and while he'd been there he'd made a large wooden puppet, Pinocchio, which was to be the key to his fortune on the street. Unfortunately Pinocchio had become a bit battered on his journey down to Siracusa and several repairs were called for, his nose having to be glued back on and a new wig made. Once the repairs had been done, Manny realized that he had a new problem, since the strings weren't too easy to control and occasionally Pinocchio's head would be whipped off by accident when he was supposed to be nodding. Then Manny and Antonio came to the conclusion that even more money could be made if they manufactured small Pinocchios out of papier-mâché and sold them on the street at Christmas. Accordingly, they went out to collect loads of newspapers and set to work tearing them into little pieces and leaving them to soak in bowls of water, but then they got sidetracked by the immediate need to go out begging for money to go to the wine house, and after that the Pincchio project was forgotten and the papier-mâché dried up and had to be thrown away.

Peter and I worked with the pavement pictures and sometimes I got orders for portraits in charcoal, which I did in the sunshine outside the cave. We never made more than enough to get by but it was adequate for our needs. Antonio, who also hated begging, did odd jobs in the church for Padre Rufino, who spoke fluent Spanish and loved any opportunity of using it. Most people begged and made very much more money as a result. Although life continued on a fairly even keel, for one reason or another, quarrels started to break out much more frequently than before and the atmosphere wasn't as happy-go-lucky as it had been formerly. The arguments usually involved Salvatore, who became provocative and arrogant when he was drunk. He was a junkie, and regularly scrounged beer and cigarettes off people but never contributed anything in the way of food or drink himself, as well as avoiding payment for his share of the meals by saying he wasn't hungry, and then immediately finishing up what was left over instead of leaving it for people to eat in the evening. His behaviour annoyed everybody and infuriated Antonio, who sometimes had to be restrained from attacking him physically. Peter and I always found that the best way to deal with Salvatore was to ignore him completely, but it wasn't always easy.

Gerhardt and Wolfgang each brought a puppy home one day and lavished food and affection on the little animals, but a week later, for no apparent reason, Gerhardt's puppy died suddenly. We had a little funeral, Antonio digging the grave and Salvatore making a wooden cross for the little creature, but Gerhardt was inconsolable, booing away like a baby. There seemed nothing that we could do to help until Wolfgang went out and found a tiny black and white kitten, which he brought back to Gerhardt who looked at it, smiled cautiously, hiccuped and immediately adopted the little animal and forgot his bereavement. Carlo, who still visited the cave regularly, was certain that the puppy's death was due to the fact that it hadn't been inoculated, so the rest of us clubbed together to enable Wolfgang to take his pet to the vet, and luckily she thrived.

At the beginning of December the weather took a turn for the worse, the rain pouring down the hillside above the cave and turning the entrance into a river. There was a bitter wind as well and, although it wasn't too bad inside the cave, I had to wear so many layers of clothing to keep warm that I resembled a Michelin man, my movements being so restricted that I found it difficult to work on my pavement pictures. When the Santa Lucia festival started, the rain prevented us working outside the Dome but Padre Rufino invited us to make our pictures in the covered entrance to his church. We were in competition with Giacomo, a Sicilian beggar with a grizzled black beard and a voice like a rasp, but even though his presence prevented us from making as much money as we would have liked, he was adept at keeping the gypsies away. Peter and I both liked Giacomo. He usually begged at a supermarket further down the road from where I worked, and every now and then he would leave his post outside the supermarket to see how I was getting on, and if it was especially cold he would go to a bar

125

nearby and come back with a plastic cup of coffee, handing it to me without a word and stomping off to his post again. He was an excellent beggar, making far more money than I did, and I think he felt sorry for me because he loved my pictures and felt that people ought to be more generous. On one occasion, after gazing at my picture for a few minutes, he 'hrrmphed' gruffly, picked up my collecting bowl with its few thousand lire in it, and stomped off, returning about half an hour later with a gap-toothed grin on his rugged face and the bowl overflowing with cash, which he handed to me triumphantly, once more without a word.

A week before Christmas, Peter told me that he wanted us to go on a brief tour with his Santa Claus outfit, so we took the train to Reggio, passing the fires and lava flowing down Mount Etna after the eruption of the previous day, and headed straight for our favourite wine house on the far side of the railway line. Most of Reggio's usual vagabond community were congregated there, including some new faces – Raymond and Marco – whom I'd often heard mentioned. Naturally work was out of the question that evening as we were both enjoying ourselves far too much but, as Peter said, 'no problem, Baby-Prue, we have time'. We slept in the shack with Wolle, who was on his own, and next morning we went into a wine house in town to see Peter's Sicilian friends, with the idea of changing into his costume later on to make a tour of the shops. In contrast to the rain and cold of Siracusa, Reggio was so hot and sunny that it seemed totally unsuitable to be dressed up as Father Christmas, besides which we saw two other Father Christmases roaming the streets, so we spent a merry morning in the wine house instead. After lunch in the Mensa we had a siesta in the park, and then Peter felt in the mood to do his Father Christmas round which, with his triangle and off-key rendering of 'Jingle Bells', earned a great deal of money in a short time. We spent one more night with Wolle and next morning we went back to Messina and caught the train to Siracusa.

When we arrived at the cave we found, to our great joy, that Andy and Pauly were there to stay for Christmas, and Mario turned up the same evening, this time with Lutz. It was just like old times again, the cave full of people, and everyone in the mood to sing,

126

talk and play yahtzee together. In the morning Peter and I got a summons from Padre Rufino to help construct a life-size Holy Grotto, Peter being needed to construct the building out of huge polystyrene blocks, while I did the figures of the Holy Family on paper, which were later mounted on thick polystyrene sheets. We worked on this during the day, but our evenings were free for Peter to dress up as Father Christmas and go to the different parts of the town, as we'd done the previous year, to make our Christmas money.

We had been befriended by a Signora Rita who worked in a gambling club owned by her extremely dodgy brother-in-law, and she was most distressed when she heard that we lived in a cave. Early on Christmas Eve, she turned up unexpectedly with her effeminate nephew, Beppe, both of them loaded with plates, glasses and cutlery for everybody, which they deposited on the table and hurried off, waving away our thanks and wishing us all a Merry Christmas. When Peter and I called in to see her later in the day, we found that she'd prepared two large plastic bags full of beer and fruit juices for us to take back with us, and she seemed quite distraught that she couldn't give us more. She cared a lot for those less fortunate than herself and whenever we saw her after that, we always came away with some little gift.

On Christmas Eve, the main celebration for all Germans, Peter did the cooking, starting us off with some hors d'oeuvres consisting of all sorts of meat, cheese and little savoury titbits, followed by pasta with mussels in a garlic sauce, his speciality, and in addition to the wine and beer, there was a variety of spirits and liqueurs. The party got predictably lively, the loud babble of voices and laughter echoing round the cave and the evening ending up with a resounding singsong. Peter and I dragged ourselves reluctantly away just before midnight (and I had to prevail upon him not to don his Father Christmas costume), as Padre Rufino had told us firmly that he expected us to be at the Mass to see the result of our labours. He and his assistants had arranged the Holy Grotto so well that it looked surprisingly lifelike, and I was glad that we'd made the effort to go down as it filled me with the self-righteous glow that comes from knowing that one has done one's duty.

We had an unusually hearty breakfast on Christmas morning of coffee, bread, salami and olives left over from the night before, followed by gluwein to get us into the right frame of mind for our impending Christmas dinner. We had been invited out by a small group of social workers, and shortly after midday, we heard a tooting of horns in the road, where three cars waited to take us up to the schoolhouse where the feast had been prepared. There were three ladies to welcome us, all as friendly and relaxed as if they regularly entertained beggars such as us. In fact one of the women, we learned later, specialized in dealing with alcoholics and we were soon at our ease. Possibly due to the absence of alcohol we were all a bit tongue-tied at first, but it wasn't long before they got us chatting, Antonio, especially, being in his element as he was a great talker and clearly revelled in his captive audience of three women. We were given plates piled high with pasta, chicken and salad, but to start with there was only water on the table, and it wasn't until some bottles of sparkling wine were brought in that the men really started to enjoy themselves. When the second lot of wine was brought in, the conversation got going in earnest with everyone wanting to join in, even Bernd, whose command of Italian was negligible. There were cakes to end up with and when people could eat and drink no more, all the leftovers were placed in plastic bags for us to take away when we left, plus several more bottles of sparkling wine and a Christmas present of 10,000 lire each. The hospital where Big Lupo was interned was fairly close by, and we asked if we might be allowed to stop off on the way back, to see him. The social workers couldn't have been kinder or more obliging, ferrying us to the hospital, waiting while we chatted to him and then taking us back home to the cave, dismissing our thanks with 'it was a pleasure'.

Antonio, Gerhardt, Salvatore and Wolfgang went off to continue carousing in a bar, but the rest of us were content to stay in the cave as there was so much to eat and drink, and we could relax in comfort, all of us in the mood for a bit of storytelling and chat and singing while Mario played his guitar and Peter played his kazoo. It was the sort of noisy, happy evening I loved and we were all having a wonderful time, recounting experiences, cracking jokes and laughing, when all of a sudden Antonio came back, very drunk and extremely aggressive.

He proceeded to pick an argument with Little Lupo over something quite trivial, whereupon Lupo foolishly retaliated and Antonio tried to drag him out of his chair to beat him up. That failed as Lupo refused to move so, shouting insults all the while, Antonio grabbed a carving knife off the table and slashed wildly at him, narrowly missing my face as he did so. As quick as lightning Peter and Pauly leapt out of their seats, disarming Antonio and throwing him bodily out of the cave. Meanwhile Andy, Manny and I sat in a solemn row on the sofa, somewhat bemused by this uncalled-for display of violence, shaking our heads disapprovingly, tutting and saying how things weren't as they used to be. Antonio reappeared abruptly, hurling abuse at Little Lupo and making another grab for the knife, and this time it was the normally placid Andy who felled him with a rugby tackle. By now screaming curses at all of us, Antonio was dragged out of the cave by Peter and Mario and told to stay away for good, and to reinforce the message, his pack and sleeping-bag were thrown out after him as well. We heard him go down the hill, his shouts getting fainter until they could be heard no more, and then we all sat down and talked it over. Peter was very upset by this incident and said that it was time to leave the cave and we'd go to Spain for the rest of the winter. Mario and Lutz said that they would accompany us as far as Reggio as they, too, were tired of the perpetual squabbling which had culminated in such unpleasantness on Christmas Day of all days, and Manny said that he would go back to Austria with Andy and Pauly, because for him this was the final straw.

Next morning we packed our rucksacks and left the cave, bidding everybody a very fond farewell as we had no idea when we'd be back. Lupo was especially sad to see us go as he'd got on better with Peter than with anybody else, and he feared that it would be a long time before we met again. I didn't mind leaving the people so much because I was looking forward to seeing Spain, but I was sad at the thought of leaving Goliath who, at twelve years old, was getting so long in the tooth that I feared he wouldn't last much longer. My only consolation was that he had Little Lupo to care for him. I felt disillusioned that Christmas had ended as it did as I had wanted to stay in the cave until the New Year started, but Peter was unbending. We stopped by for a last drink at Russo's and found Mario and Lutz already in session, so we joined them, feeling very much jollier by the time we eventually got to the station and boarded the train for Reggio Calabria.

11   The Spanish Experience

When we arrived in Reggio the four of us and the dogs took the long route round to the wine house near the railway lines, Mario's massive girth making it too difficult for him to either climb through or over the railings. He talked seriously to Peter, trying to dissuade him from going to Spain as the last time he'd been there himself, he'd found it difficult to make money on the street and got the impression that the Spanish were becoming more intolerant of vagabonds because of their tourist trade. He feared that when we got there we'd never make the money to come back. Marco, a clean-shaven and rather opinionated German I'd met on our Father Christmas tour, agreed with him. Peter listened and acknowledged that they could be right, but said that it made no difference since we wouldn't be working on the street for long as he intended to get us jobs with his Chinese friend's circus. That was the first time I'd heard about it but it perked me up a lot as I looked forward to working in a circus again. I questioned him eagerly: what was the name of the circus and where was it based? Was it one of the many circuses we'd come across in Italy? Peter admitted that he couldn't remember either his friend's name or that of the circus but since his friend was a German-speaking Chinaman with a beautiful Spanish wife, he didn't think he would be too hard to trace, the circus grapevine being what it was.

Of course we had a more immediate problem and that was to make money for the journey as Peter wanted to leave the next day; but he collected assiduously for me while I worked on the pavement with my pictures and then went to beg at a little church he knew. We spent the night with Thomas, a good-hearted but unrelaxed character with a permanently fierce expression and a tendency to know best. We had breakfast with him in his well-kept squat the following morning and, glaring at us pugnaciously as was his wont, he presented us with a bottle of sparkling wine to be opened at midnight on New Year's Eve, wherever we happened to be.

After another hard day's work and lunch at the Mensa, we took the train to Crotone. That was a lucky town for us and we found that working as Madonnaros, we made even more money than by selling my watercolours, and took the train to Giola di Colle feeling reasonably affluent. We'd done well there on our last visit and, being Sunday, we weren't disappointed on this occasion, with Peter begging at the church where Wolfgang had been, and I making a picture on the pavement outside the church we'd worked at before. Afterwards we went back to the bar where the people had been so welcoming, and we found that they remembered us and greeted us like old friends, buying us one drink after another so that by the time we got on the night train to Forli, we slept so soundly that even the ticket collector had trouble in rousing us. Financially we didn't do quite so well in Forli this time, partly because the period after Christmas was always rather sluggish money-wise, and partly due to the presence of a crowd of gypsies and other beggars giving us unexpected competition. So we travelled on to Faenza and then to Imola, where we did a lot better, Peter selling several of my watercolours as I worked on the pavement; and on New Year's Eve we were in Bologna, sitting in the crowded railway station and waiting for our train to Alissandria as we toasted 1992 with Thomas's bottle of wine.

We arrived in Alissandria very early in the morning, having had very little sleep and not feeling at our best. We found a bar to thaw out in, the weather outside being distinctly chilly, and then, still early, we trailed into town to a church at which we'd been told there was to be a special Mass in honour of the Virgin Mary. It was an ideal opportunity to make money, so I got to work on a picture while Peter collected for me and, despite the presence of three Arab beggars in front of the church door, by lunchtime we'd made

132

more than enough to continue our journey. We had something to eat and went to Novi, where Peter said they never closed the centrally heated station waiting room and where we bedded down for the night after spending a congenial evening in a cosy little wine house. Spreading our sleeping-bags out on the floor, we were both so tired by this time, as we hadn't even had our siesta, that we slept right through until the trains started running in the morning, unaware of other travellers in the waiting room and having to be awakened by two jovial railway policemen. One of them threw open the window to let in some fresh air while the other shook Peter, not ungently, to rouse him from his slumber.

'Hello, hello, what's all this then? Come on folks, up you get, this isn't a hotel you know.'

There were several amused people in the waiting room and we joined in the general laughter, apologizing for our presence as we hastily brushed ourselves down and rolled up our sleeping-bags. We took the train to Genoa, but it started to rain and we made so little money in the covered walkway that we decided to carry on to Savona. It stopped raining there and we did slightly better with my pictures, but it wasn't until Peter found a supermarket to beg at that we made any significant amount of money. We spent the night under a hedge in the railway station gardens, the weather having improved enormously, and the following morning we took the train to the pretty little seaside town of Alassio. Unfortunately we were beaten to it work-wise, as another Madonnaro had arrived there before us with his caravanette, two children and a dog, so we took the train to Imperia, a lovely city as well as the cleanest I'd ever come across in Italy. Peter found me a good place to work in the old town and stressed the importance of making the money for our tickets through to Spain because experience had taught him that we'd be unlikely to do well in France. The people of Imperia were outstandingly generous and by working hard all day with Peter collecting for me, as well as selling three of the finished pictures, we made the money to buy our tickets to Barcelona, with some to spare.

Peter, full of nostalgia for his Foreign Legion days, wanted to stop off in Marseilles to revisit his old haunts. He took me to where he used to go drinking in the dock area, and in one of the bars there I was thrilled to see, for the first time, a couple of Legionnaires, immaculate in their uniform and white kepis. We went from one bar to another, all very different; some with a military atmosphere, some with predominantly Arab clientele, and the one we ended up in, warm and friendly and full of Africans. I liked Marseilles, which didn't seem anywhere near as sleazy as I'd expected, but Peter said that he had no intention of spending the night there, sleeping rough as we were, so we took the train to Aubagne, an attractive little garrison town where he'd done his training. Again we went on a tour of all the bars he knew from the past, and he found out, among other things, that his Captain Ivanov, of whom I'd heard so many tales, was stationed at the garrison in Aubagne. Peter was excited and, hoping that by chance they might run into each other, he easily persuaded me to delay our journey for a few days.

We found an empty goods-wagon at the railway station to sleep in, and during the day I made pictures in front of a supermarket. The weather got worse, becoming bitterly cold and making it difficult to sleep at night, in addition to which we made barely enough money to survive, a problem that Peter had expected. We met three French beggars who lived in the goods-wagon next to ours, and they lent us a thick blanket which made all the difference to our comfort at night. They were nice lads and invited us for a meal in their wagon, which they'd made quite homely with posters all over the walls, and they advised us to beg in the normal way if we wanted to make money, instead of wasting our time with the pictures. Peter tried that next morning, but as there were other beggars in town as well as the three young men, he didn't do very well and decided that it was better to collect for me. We stayed for two more days but it continued to be hard work making enough money to survive and Peter was further discouraged because he hadn't run across his Captain Ivanov.

We saw no reason to stay any longer and took the overnight train to Barcelona and, after the freezing chill of France, we were suddenly basking in warm sunshine. Business was less than brilliant but we made enough money to get us as far as Tarragona, where Peter located a good wine house and we each had an enormous omelette-filled roll each. We didn't do too well with our pavement pictures there either, and it began to look as if Mario had been right, but after our first night in a goods-wagon, we discovered that there was an excellent free hostel in the town which provided beds for the night, hot showers and three meals a day. We stayed there for two days of luxury and learned that the social services in Spain were first-class, and almost every town provided a free meal, a bed, or a ticket to the next town. We could have stayed for a third night in the hostel in Tarragona, but as we were making so little money on the street, Peter felt that we might just as well move on and see if business was better in a smaller town, as was usually the case in Italy. He also wanted to be on the move to look out for his Chinese friend's circus.

We travelled south to Tortosa and, for the first time since leaving Italy, we started to do well with our pavement pictures. It was a charming old town, with a pedestrian precinct along which everybody passed and where I spread out all my pictures, and as soon as I started work people paused to watch and to throw down money. In addition to my collection of religious pictures, I had done a couple of pretty ladies in eighteenth century costume and to my surprise the people loved them. Peter sold them for 1000 pesetas each which represented a fair sum of money to us as the cost of living was less than in Italy. He also got me two more orders for pretty ladies in costume, and after finishing work in the evening we had a meal in a cheap restaurant and then went to a wine house that Peter's unerring nose had located. I thought that the Spanish wine was delicious and I loved their food, which was presented so enticingly in the bars that it was often impossible to resist. The weather was so balmy that we spent the night out in the open, on a hill overlooking the town, and next day the good weather continued and so did business, becoming brisker as people got to know that we were there and wanted to order pictures from us. All good things come to an end, however, and that evening two policemen arrived to tell us that we couldn't work there without a licence. They were very nice about it and allowed me to stay for the rest of the evening, but said that they didn't want to see us there the following day unless we had the licence, and as that proved unnecessarily expensive, we moved on south to Sagunto.

Although we wanted to avoid the big towns, Peter had seen advertisements for a circus in Valencia, so we stopped off there to see if we could glean any information as to the whereabouts of his friend. It should have been a comparatively simple matter but the problem in our case was Peter's inability to remember either the name of his friend or that of the circus, only that the man was a German-speaking Chinaman with a beautiful Spanish wife. Naturally enough, nobody at the circus in Valencia could help us, so we had to content ourselves with a free meal at the municipal canteen, after which we spent a few unrewarding hours on the pavement before seeking solace in a wine house.

We continued our journey south on the coastal railway line, avoiding the biggest towns where possible and always keeping an eye open for posters advertising circuses but getting no closer to locating Peter's Chinese friend. In every town we stopped at, Peter would help me to stick my pictures down onto the pavement, and once I'd got started he would go off in search of the social services to see if there was a free canteen, or to get tickets for bocadillos, those huge rolls filled with almost anything one wanted, that we'd first experienced in Tarragona.

In Sueca we were given bocadillos in addition to tickets for Gandia, which would have been a good town to beg in, but was less good from our viewpoint as the pavements were so narrow that there was no room for my pictures and we had to make do with a space just off the main street where there were few passers-by. We were doing surprisingly well, in fact, until we were joined by an extremely drunk but very humorous young Scot, who settled himself down on his rucksack to talk to us, every now and again shouting raucously at people to put their money down, which had the reverse effect. I enjoyed his company because he made me laugh so much and it was a nice change to be able to communicate properly in my own language, but Peter found his presence highly embarrassing while he was trying to make money, so he stalked off to the wine house. The young man left eventually and I resumed work on my own, profitably once more.

We carried on to Tavernes which was full of nice people and a good town money-wise, but the railway station was a long bus-ride from the town centre and we had to find a place to sleep other than our usual goods-wagon. The building sites were so thoroughly enclosed that in the end we had to make do with the porchway to the entrance to a block of flats. This was not an ideal sleeping place as, although it was sheltered from the weather, it was very much in the public eye and we were awoken by people stepping over us as they emerged from the flats to go to work in the morning. With all his years of experience on the road, Peter was used to minor inconveniences like this, even finding them amusing, but although I tried hard to appear the seasoned vagabond, I found it exceedingly embarrassing to climb out of my sleeping-bag with curious people wandering by. I also felt terribly conspicuous when we were collecting cardboard boxes to sleep on, going through the garbage containers late at night and then walking along the road with a pile of them flattened out and ready for use. Fortunately Peter usually did the cardboard box run, leaving me at our chosen site with the rucksacks.

We travelled on down to Benefaio, where we found a bar owned by a lovely family who, more often than not, refused payment for the food and wine that they gave us, as well as giving us all sorts of advice as to where we could make money. I did portraits of them, the only way we could express our appreciation of their kindness without causing offence. They insisted that we stay for the festival of their patron saint, San Antonio, a charming, homely festival and very different to the ones we were used to in Italy. After the procession with the clergy and the brass bands, the people of the town all brought their pets along to be blessed by the Bishop – horses, dogs, donkeys, goats, cats, numerous cage-birds, tortoises and even goldfish, the gypsy children bringing chickens or cockerels with ribbons tied round their necks for the occasion. When all that was over, a free meal had been prepared for everybody in the town – freshly baked bread and a thick soup of chicken and rice, which people collected in bowls or saucepans to take home with them. When the food had all been distributed, the streets cleared like magic as everybody disappeared, and that was the end of the festival.

Our next stop was Xativa where the free canteen was seriously below par and Peter found a cheap restaurant for us to eat in instead. From the business point of view it was passable and we had a cosy railway-wagon to sleep in, but when someone told us that there was a festival in Mogenta, a few stops down the line, we went there to see if we could do a little bit better. Unfortunately for us our informant had got it wrong, and not only was there no festival, but the town was so small that we could find nowhere suitable to work. We discussed the problem with a fat and jolly policeman who suggested that we try our luck at La Encina, so off we went again, thanking him profusely for his help, only to realize that he was a Spanish practical joker because, if we'd thought Mogenta was small, it was a city in comparison to La Encina.

We found ourselves at a tiny railway station in the middle of nowhere, with a two and a half hour's wait for the next train south. Peter, by this time was very much in need of liquid refreshment, and asked the station master if there was a bar nearby. We were directed across the railway line and told that we would come to a road and we would be able to see the bar from there. It was pitch dark by now, but we crossed the line as directed and scrambled down the bank, coming to a dirt road, and sure enough we could see some lights in the distance. Eagerly we hurried along, our faces falling to discover that it was only a man fixing his tractor by lamplight, but we were redirected to go back the way we'd come, cross some fields and there we would find the main road, from where we'd see the bar. Back we went into the darkness, stumbling through the fields until at last we came to a main road, and there, only a short way ahead, we saw the welcome sign, 'Bar'. In fact it was a hotel and looked expensive, but it wasn't and we were able to afford a plate of food to go with our wine and when we'd finished, Peter put his few remaining coins into a fruit machine and won 5,000 pesetas. It was a windfall.

We got back to the station only just in time to leap onto the Intercity train as it was about to pull out. We had no tickets but it didn't matter as no ticket collector came and we sat in comfort and watched 'Rocky 2' on the video until we came to Alicante. We all had to get out there, so we spent the rest of the night in a goods-wagon, the next morning taking the first train to Murcia, a medium-sized town at the end of the coastal railway line. We knew that if we wanted to go any further south we would have to travel inland first, so we thought it better to talk it over before coming to a decision. We'd been travelling almost non-stop for the last six weeks and, apart from feeling dirty all the time, we were tired of humping our rucksacks around with us and having to search for a sleeping place every night. We liked Spain but there seemed no likelihood of ever coming across Peter's friend's circus and, with many months of winter still to come, we wanted to be somewhere settled so that we could relax. Peter suggested that we go back to Siracusa and he would find somewhere for us to live on our own, away from other people's problems.

I needed no persuasion even though I preferred the Spanish wine. Peter knew of a hostel in Murcia where we could eat, sleep and shower, so as soon as we'd finished work we hurried along to it, to arrive in time for the evening meal. There was a massive crowd of people outside, all waiting for the doors to open, and while we were there the police came round to do a random check and dragged two young men away with them. The dinner was good and plentiful, and afterwards I was taken round to the women's hostel while Peter went off to the men's quarters. I seemed to be the only woman there apart from a couple of elderly crones who were sitting in the reception room and cackling away to each other, and I was allowed to have a bath rather than a shower, after which I went to my dormitory and slept soundly until I was awoken by someone in a nurse's uniform. At breakfast I realized that this must have been an old people's home because all the other women looked extremely ancient and in varying degrees of senility, and by the way they knew and abused each other, they were obviously long-term residents. We were given milk and biscuits and there was a minor fracas as one old woman tried to steal her neighbour's biscuit and got herself attacked by another old lady with a broom, but it was all very entertaining.

I met Peter and we took the train to Orihuele which, like Murcia, was a good town in which to make money, but which also had the same stinking river flowing through, except that in Orihuele I was working within whiffing distance. There was an excellent canteen at the geriatric hospital, where I had to do a picture for someone, surrounded by senile old men gibbering at me as they all crowded round to watch me work. On our journey northwards we stopped at several different towns to test them for possible future visits to Spain. Elx was lovely and very good work-wise, Elda was unexceptional, and by the time we reached Villeva the weather got so bad – wet and violently windy – that we found it impossible to work. It was Sunday evening when we stopped at Villa Reale and the weather had improved, but no sooner had we started work on the pavement outside a church than three Spanish beggars arrived and told us to move on, all of them very drunk, abusive and extremely aggressive. Discretion being the better part of valour, we packed up our work and made as dignified a retreat as possible, hoping fervently that the three beggars would be cursed with piles and ingrowing toenails.

I must say that even apart from that incident, our return journey was less fortuitous than it might have been. We earned enough money to eat and drink in comfort, although Peter wasted an undue amount in the fruit machines which were a feature of every bar, but the weather deteriorated badly and at Tarragona, where we had hoped to spend the night in the hostel and have a much-needed hot shower, we were told that travellers could only stay there every two months, and we'd been there only six weeks previously. So we travelled on to Cambrils and found an adequate sleeping place in the porch of an abandoned house, leaving our rucksacks there while we went in search of cardboard boxes and coming back to find that a cat had crapped on our sleeping-bags, very cleverly managing to soil both of them.

'Oh, bull shit,' said Peter with feeling.

'No, cat shit,' I corrected him as I cleaned it off with loathing, and for some reason we both had a fit of uncontrollable giggles which left us both feeling a lot better.

At Vila Nova, which was another good town for work, we slept in an empty goods-wagon and were awoken with a jolt in the early hours of the morning as our wagon got hitched to an engine, and we had to leap out to avoid being carried off to some unknown destination, spending the rest of the night in an uncomfortable burnt-out car. At Barcelona a dog lifted its leg against Peter's rucksack, and wherever we tried to find a place to sleep we were moved on by the police, only not as polite and friendly as we'd encountered elsewhere. We stopped at Macanet, where we hoped to make money as it looked a good-sized town on the map, but it was only a railway junction, and when we arrived in Girona, the heavens opened and we got drenched. Our last stop in Spain was better, Figueres, where the sun came out and we had no difficulty in making the money to get to Perpignon in France. From there we train-hopped most of the way to Ventimiglia, arriving with not a coin to our names. Peter was in his element, however, on home territory as it were, and within an hour of tramping round the restaurants and bars, he'd sold a picture to a policeman and we were once more solvent.

It was now almost the end of February and desperately cold in the north of Italy, with such an icy wind in Alassio that I could scarcely work, as my fingers got so numb. But, town by town, we made our way towards Sicily and the further south we came, the warmer it got. At last we reached Reggio Calabria, basking in glorious sunshine, just over two months after we'd left, and the first person we ran into was Mario, astonished and delighted to see us back so soon when he'd been convinced that once we got to Spain we'd be stranded there. We had a good reason to celebrate that night and the following morning we took the ferry to Messina.

12 The Cave in the Cactus Ring

As soon as we arrived in Siracusa we hurried along to Signor Russo's wine house to have some refreshment before he closed, and saw, sitting outside with Little Lupo and Bernd, none other than Goliath, looking fat and sleek and showing no signs of age as he raced up the road to greet us. We stood outside in the sunshine, drinking beer and catching up on each other's news. Andy and Pauly had gone back to Austria and Gerhardt had also left, but Big Lupo was out of hospital and Uwe had returned from Palermo after more than a year's absence, so there were now seven of them living in the cave. We all walked back together and I had a joyful reunion with Big Lupo and Manny, who told me, chuckling richly, that he kept meaning to leave but he just hadn't got around to it yet.

Uwe

I was introduced to Uwe, whom I had already met in Palermo apparently, but I didn't remember him and it surprised me, because we hit it off immediately. He was a big man, heavy, and even ugly in a kind sort of way, with long, fair hair and a beard, and a soft American drawl when he wasn't speaking German. He had a droll sense of humour and kept me in fits of laughter with his little comments on people and life in general. Although Salvatore was still living in the cave, he seemed a lot more restrained and the whole atmosphere had improved noticeably since we'd been away, which, Wolfgang told us, was due to the fact that anyone creating a disturbance now had to buy a crate of beer for the people. It felt so good to be back and to be able to relax after all our travelling, although Peter made it clear that he wanted to find a place for just the two of us.

Two days later he took me to see an abandoned house that he'd found. It was beside the railway line, not far from the cave, and he'd discovered that it had been declared uninhabitable after the previous year's earthquake. There were cracks all over the walls and ceilings, with fallen plaster and debris everywhere, but there was a lot of old furniture left inside and it seemed ideal for us. There was a restaurant across the road, so we asked the owner if we would be allowed to occupy the house and were told that he would be only too glad of our presence, as he was supposed to be keeping an eye on the place and we would be a deterrent to the vandals who were always breaking in. I didn't much like the sound of that but Peter assured me that nobody would bother us once it was known that we were living inside. We decided that the first floor was in the best repair, as well as being light and airy, so we set about cleaning it and throwing out all the rubble. We were left with an apartment that was positively palatial by our standards, with a bedroom, a dining room and a kitchen, almost fully furnished, and even a bathroom. There was no running water but there was a tap outside, so we didn't have to go far to fill the water canisters.

We stayed there for a blissful week and I painted watercolours by day with the luxury of a big table and plenty of light, going into town with Peter after our siesta to make money with my pavement pictures, while on our way home from the wine house we would usually stop by at the cave for a game of yahtzee and some cheery gossip. But it all came to an end when the brother of the restaurant-owner marched in one morning while I was working, without even knocking, and informed me that we would have to leave at once as he had no authority to let us stay. I was somewhat taken aback by his officious manner, but he bade me continue with my painting and

144

stalked round the apartment, muttering 'humph' every now and again, and seemed impressed by what we'd done. When Peter arrived the man told us that as we were obviously responsible people, and on condition we cleaned the rest of the house, he would allow us, as a special favour, to stay on but not in that particular apartment, which he wanted for one of his workers, but in the one below. Peter coldly declined his offer and we moved back to the cave.

Little Lupo suggested we have a look at the caves that they used to live in several years before. They'd been evicted because the dogs bothered the school children using the public footpath, but as we had no animals we weren't likely to have any problems and as far as he knew the caves were still habitable. He took us across the area of common land to the other side of the footpath, where there was a rocky outcrop further up the hill. There, hidden by some trees, a bramble thicket and masses of huge cacti, were two caves, one of them far too big for our purposes, but a smaller one next door which was absolutely perfect. The entrance had been walled up to leave only a doorway and we learned later that it had been inhabited by a Sicilian family more than thirty years before. The rocky ground projected out on either side, forming a natural court-yard that had once been tiled and was still in good condition. Beyond that were two trees, and a ring of massive cacti and bram-bles enclosed a natural garden, full of wild flowers. The view over-looked the rocky terrain between the caves and, beyond the Mormon Church and some blocks of flats, the sea could be seen sparkling in the sunshine. It was idyllic!

'Oh, Peter, I love it!' I exclaimed. 'I couldn't imagine anywhere nicer to live.'

He laughed at my delight and agreed, and we spent all the following day clearing out the rubble and rocks from the inside. Peter hung a wooden door which could be locked, erected some shelves and made a table and, after finding a double-bed frame with a mattress, we moved in. I should explain that in Italy people discard all kinds of perfectly good furniture and other household items so there was never any difficulty in setting up house – it was just a matter of going around the town and finding what had been dumped at all the garbage containers. Over the days that followed we acquired other pieces of furniture: a gas cooker with a working oven; a three-legged settee which Peter repaired; a wooden chest for our clothes and for use as an extra seat, and a little chest of drawers. Signora Rita gave us all manner of essential pots, pans, crockery and cutlery, and even a brand new duvet.

We had the most glorious few weeks on our own, sometimes going down to the big cave to socialize with the men, while on other occasions the more energetic of them would visit us. Bernd never made it, and Manny gave up after a few visits because he seemed unable to negotiate the rocky and uneven path without falling over or getting lost in the undergrowth. We would hear a hollering and go outside to see him standing in the midst of a cactus thicket, waving helplessly for someone to come and rescue him. Bernd persuaded Peter to take one of the kittens that his cat had produced, although I tried to dissuade him in view of our unstable way of life. Peter waved aside my objections, gaily assuring me that he would train Felix (for that was to be his name) to get used to traffic and people, so that he could travel with us. I wasn't to worry. Felix turned out to be female, a pretty tortoiseshell, and though he wouldn't change her name, Peter regularly took her down to the wine house tucked inside his shirt, and she had no fear of the noisy outside world. I loved her, but Peter was always her favourite.

As Easter approached we all took the opportunity to make extra money, Peter and I going into the town morning and evening to work on the pavement, almost always selling the finished product. Wolfgang and Manny thought of a new way of raising funds, more fun and more productive than the usual begging. They had found a discarded pushchair and strolled through the town with Wolfgang squashed into the seat, dressed as a baby with an outsize nappy, a frilly bonnet, a dummy and holding out the begging bowl, making unintelligible sounds while Manny pushed him along wearing an apron, a woman's hat and his beaming smile.

One evening after work when Peter and I were wandering along to Russo's wine house, he suddenly stopped me and called out to a tall man with his back to us in a tobacconist's shop.

'Irish Pete! Hey, fucker!'

The man turned around sharply and his face broke into a grin.

'Peter! Long time no see, man! What are you doing here? Where are you staying?'

Peter had often talked about this man who had twinkling blue eyes, black hair curling to his shoulders, a thick moustache and a strong Liverpool accent. He paid for his cigarettes and joined us on the pavement, introducing us to Karina, a sour-looking German girl who was

Irish Pete

holding on to a large dog. Pausing for a few drinks at the wine house, we walked up the hill to our cave, the two men talking non-stop, obviously revelling in each other's company. Irish Pete had a bottle of whisky with him, which he insisted on sharing with us. I observed that he didn't sound very Irish to me and he confessed, laughing, that he'd been brought up in a children's home in Liverpool but that he had an Irish passport. He said that he liked the look of Siracusa and thought he might stay around for a while if he could find a good squat.

Peter showed them the cave next door, and although Karina was less enthusiastic, Irish Pete decided that it was ideal for the two of them and the dog. Next day he set about clearing out the rubble and making it habitable, laying a carpet on the floor and furnishing it with other bits and pieces that he found around the town. As they had only a small camping-gas cooker, Peter invited them to eat with us since it was as easy to cook for four people as for two. Karina showed little appreciation of the efforts that Irish Pete made to provide her with a comfortable home, nagging at him constantly in German and keeping to herself most of the time. I suggested that we take her down to the big cave so that she got a chance to talk to other people in her own language, even though she'd been uncommunicative with Peter himself. He couldn't stand her and found it impossible to comprehend how such a 'fine man' as Irish Pete could tolerate living with such a shrew. Karina soon got very friendly with the men in the big cave and took to spending more and more time with them, eventually moving down there permanently with her dog. If Irish Pete was offended he didn't show it and our mealtimes were much more enjoyable without her grim countenance putting a damper on the conversation.

Not long after her departure, Pete brought home a young couple he'd met in Russo's and invited them to share his cave if they had nowhere else to go, which they did. Eric was French and played the guitar for his living while Veronica, a beautiful Italian girl, accompanied him on the flute. Felix quickly accepted their beautifully-mannered dog and soon they became regular visitors, sleeping in Irish Pete's cave and eating with us. Mario and Wolle arrived in Siracusa, but although they slept in the big cave, Mario always came to us at mealtimes. He and Eric both loved cooking and took it in turns with Peter to produce all sorts of delectable meals, and after work in the evenings they would sit round our courtyard, often joined by Little Lupo and Uwe, to play their guitars and sing, Uwe revealing a talent for playing the most poignant blues on a mouth organ.

Carlo visited us regularly, and when Peter bought some dice and made a board, we introduced Eric and Veronica to the pleasures of yahtzee, to which they rapidly became addicted, so that when work was over they wanted nothing so much as to tempt us into a game. Meanwhile Irish Pete struck up a close friendship with Uwe, with whom he had a wonderful rapport, and the two of them took to going out carousing nearly every evening, frequently lurching back to our cave late at night to continue the party. Peter, usually so good-natured, tended to become very irascible at these intrusions and I can't say they pleased me overmuch either. We were finding it increasingly irksome to have people around all the time wanting to make merry, with never a moment to ourselves. While we weren't unsociable, the reason we'd moved out of the big cave initially was to have a bit of privacy, and we missed those first few weeks of comparative seclusion when life had been so harmonious. Yet it was difficult to dissuade people from gathering in our domain without causing offence.

Towards the end of May it became time to think about moving on as we intended to spend the summer in Kefalonia. Irish Pete wanted to stay in our cave while we were away, and we were only too glad for him to be there to look after the place. Wolfgang and his dog left Siracusa to stay with friends in Brindisi and we arranged to meet him a few weeks later, when we'd got ourselves organized for the journey and made a bit of money.

As Peter had predicted, Felix was no problem at all away from home, loving the attention she received from strangers and the frequent titbits she was offered, and sleeping a lot of the time. Our first stop was Augusta and, after working on a big picture in the square, we slept in a corner of the fish market but were awoken while it was still dark by the fishermen setting up their stalls. We went to Reggio for the day to spend time with all our friends in the various wine houses, after which we took the night train to Taranto, getting very little sleep as it was full of exuberant and noisy young servicemen returning to their bases. Taranto wasn't a good town financially, but the Mensa was excellent, we slept well in the gardens by the fishing port, and Peter ran into an old German friend with a homely, genial face, Fred Feuerstein, whom he'd often described to me as another 'old wolf of the street'. They had so much to talk about that we didn't get to Monopoli until the following evening and the only place we could find to sleep was in an alcove in the harbour wall, romantic but draughty. Next morning we started work in the market only to be moved on almost immediately by a policeman, but before we had even packed up our things, a priest came along and shepherded us up to his church to do a large picture of St Anthony on paper.

When we'd finished the priest gave us 50,000 lire for it, and meanwhile we'd made a good collection into the bargain, so we took the train to Bari feeling rather cock-a-hoop. The luck stayed with us because we found that we'd arrived in time for the festival of San Nicola, and started work on a picture that same evening. It was a very grand affair, lasting for three days, the streets lit up so magnificently that the Christmas lights of Regent Street would have looked meagre by comparison. Although I loved the atmosphere of the festival, I hated working with such huge crowds milling round me, but Peter's presence was reassuring and it was well worth the discomfort, because at the end of it all we found we'd made more than enough money for our tickets to Greece. We'd been sleeping under the sea wall by the fishing harbour, and it was a lovely place to retire to after work with our wine and roast chicken, especially on the last night when we had a perfect view of the fantastic firework display that signalled the end of the festival. Our next stop in Gioia di Colle was less fortunate. First of all the churches were almost devoid of people, the whole of the population having turned out for the funeral of a much-loved local dignitary, and second, to my intense chagrin, my rucksack was missing when we went back to the station.

'I don't *believe* it!' I stormed. 'It's the third time this has happened! Why do people always have to steal *my* pack? It's not even as if it looks smart or new or anything. It's just not fair!'

Peter soothed me down as always and found us a pretty place to sleep under a hedge covered with wild roses, and with his arms round me and Felix purring in my lap, I soon recovered my composure. After all, I thought, Peter has the sleeping bags, I have my painting things and it's more of a nuisance than anything else to have to get myself reclothed by the church before leaving.

Helmuth

We took the train to Brindisi next morning and walked down to the port, where the vagabonds gathered in the gardens after work. Sure enough there were several already there, including Helmuth whom I remembered having seen before, still pouchy-eyed and with his drooping moustache, but looking very much more affluent, plumper, well dressed and riding a little motorbike.

'It's the first time I've seen a beggar on a motorbike,' laughed Peter.

'Ah well, you know how it is,' said Helmuth, comfortably. 'I've got a good church and everybody knows me. I only work at weekends so I like to look smart.'

I was introduced to Lapsi, a thin, fair-haired man with a beard and a permanently amiable expression, and to Mahler Klaus, whom Otto had often mentioned. He was also very thin and bearded, with large, anxious eyes peering from behind thick glasses, and he spoke English well. After a few beers in the sunshine Helmuth chugged off on his motorbike and the rest of us trooped down to the little ferryboat that took us across to Casale, from where it was only a few stops on the bus to where the men lived, in what looked like derelict barracks by the military airfield.

Despite the noise of the planes, it was the most beautiful spot, in a wooded area thick with eucalyptus, fir trees and ilex oaks, amongst which the buildings were dotted, some more ruined than others. The men lived in the biggest block, which was in reasonable condition, and they each had a room of their own, curtained off from the main passageway. Peter and I were allotted one with a mattress on the floor and we dumped our things there before being taken on a tour of the place by Wolfgang, who was particularly proud of the kitchen, which was as neat as a pin and beautifully fitted out, with pans and cooking implements hanging on the walls and a fine wire mesh in the window and door to keep out the insects. There were three large dogs apart from Wolfgang's, but Felix was unperturbed by them and went off to explore on her own, finding a colony of mice in Helmuth's room which she proceeded to kill one by one, much to his delight. Bernd, a tall, black-bearded character with a doting mastiff at his heels, cooked us a tasty lunch and later we met Volker, who busked with a guitar and a Pink Panther puppet. He spoke English well too and was clean-shaven, a good-looking man with blue eyes and long blonde hair. After a short siesta Peter and I went to the Church of San Vito, where I was given a lovely assortment of clothes and underwear in a canvas holdall to replace what I'd lost. We made a leisurely detour of several bars and wine houses, and got back to the squat to find everyone gathered in Helmuth's room, some sitting round the table, some on his bed while Volker played the old campfire

151

songs on his guitar. It was like being back in the big cave in the early days, and I loved it.

Next morning Mahler Klaus asked me if he could have a look at my watercolours and was very complimentary. When he realized how long I took to produce a painting, though, he considered that I was working unprofitably and gave me a lesson in how to speed up my technique. I watched him work and was amazed by his skill and how quickly he dashed off a picture and he gave me several tips on how I could take shortcuts in my painting, which I looked forward to trying. I was told later that Klaus's main problem was his fondness for wine, and when he'd sold enough pictures he would drink happily until all the money was spent, run up a few debts here and there until he could get no more credit, upon which he would paint feverishly for a few hours until he had enough pictures to sell, at which point the cycle would start again.

We were having such fun that we stayed in the squat for about ten days. Each morning people would drift in and out of the kitchen to make coffee or tea, sitting there quietly until the desire for movement and communication seeped into the body and then, one by one, they would wend their way into Brindisi to make money, or to go shopping. Helmuth pottered around the squat most days and Lapsi loved to go sea-fishing off the rocky beach nearby. I made my pavement pictures, under no pressure to make more than enough to live for each day and without the need for Peter to collect for me, and the work became a pleasure instead of a necessary chore. I was proud of my pictures, and even if I made very little money while I worked on my own, people were always friendly and complimentary and I loved to bask in the adulation. On a couple of occasions Peter and I went into Lecce for the day, partly for the work but mainly to visit Michele's wine house and gossip with friends. Although not as lucrative as Christmas and Easter, life seemed so much easier in the summer, so much more carefree, more pleasant, and in the evenings we would all gather in Helmuth's room to talk and do Lapsi's crossword, or to sing, depending on everyone's mood. Then Otto turned up, and although it was great fun seeing him again, he was so noisy and mischievous that he annoyed Bernd into leaving the squat altogether and Peter and I felt that it was time to go to Greece.

13   The Summer Tour

As soon as we arrived at the youth hostel in Patras I wanted to try out Mahler Klaus's painting methods and in a short while, even though I hadn't completely mastered the technique, I had slashed my painting time by at least two hours per picture and could produce around seven in a day. Peter was delighted because it meant that theoretically he could cut the asking price and we'd still be in profit. When I'd finished about fifteen watercolours he mounted them on card and we went round the restaurants to see how well they sold at 1,000 drachmas each, half the original price. Even though he was dealing with the local Greeks, Peter sold six pictures in less than two hours and was triumphant as we celebrated in Mama Maria's wine house. It was time to try Kefalonia, he said, reminding me how well we'd worked last year.

I was as enthusiastic as he was to go there for the summer, so two days later we took the ferry to Sami, the pretty little port at the foot of green, pine-clad hills which curved round a sparkling blue bay, the water transparent and inviting in the hot afternoon sun. We left our packs in a cafeneion, and Felix shot up a tree outside to settle down to sleep in the branches, while we had a quick swim to cool off. We relaxed with some beers for the rest of the afternoon, and when dusk came we found a cheap taverna to have a meal before going out to sell some pictures. Even though it was the end of June there were surprisingly few tourists around, so Peter suggested that we go to Argostoli, the capital, which might be busier.

We slept on the beach, and the following day we took the bus across the island and Peter left me outside a cafeneion with a protesting Felix and went in search of a sleeping place. He came back minutes later to take us to a disused building site on the main street, where we dumped the rucksacks and Felix in one of the rooms upstairs, open but hidden from the road. He went back to the cafeneion while I gave Felix food and water, unsure of how she'd settle in such a place. I needn't have worried because once she'd finished eating, she ran downstairs into some waste ground at the back where a couple of young cats were basking in the sun. Relieved, I went to join Peter in the cafeneion where he was engrossed in watching a game of cards. I asked Lefteri and Mitso, the brothers who ran the cafeneion, if I could do some painting at one of the empty tables. They had no objection and sat me in the back room where I could work undisturbed.

They were so jolly that we came in every day and, while I did my painting, Peter would watch the old men play cards, often being invited to join a game for a small stake. People would talk to me as they watched me at work and occasionally somebody would buy me a beer, and when the cafeneion closed at lunch time, we would have a meal in a cheap restaurant nearby where the food was always hot. Feeling stuffed to bursting point, we would stagger home for a siesta in the squat, which was pleasantly airy, though dusty, and afterwards we'd go back to the cafeneion and I would do another couple of hours work. When Peter had mounted the pictures on card, my time was my own and we would have a drink together before wandering into the centre of town. There Peter would leave me in a pleasant cafeneion overlooking the harbour, to sip an ouzo and do a crossword while he went off selling on his own. He sold more pictures that way as everyone assumed that he was the artist and although he didn't correct them, it irked him. He decided to have a go at painting himself and next morning, to the amazement and curiosity of the old men, Peter sat with me instead of playing cards and painted three creditable landscapes, nothing like mine, but bright and impressionistic. He sold all three and returned to me full of jubilation but, having made his point, thereafter he rested on his laurels and happily returned to playing cards with his old men.

We had fun in Argostoli, which was essentially a Greek town even though there were a lot of tourists there. The people were friendly and always seemed to be laughing, with everybody knowing everybody else, and we received nothing but kindness while we were there. I can't say that I was keen on the squat, however, because although it was dry and fairly sheltered, I couldn't do my painting there and I didn't particularly like leaving Felix for so much of the day. After the natural beauty of our cave, and even the squat in Brindisi, the building site seemed so dreary and I felt I was missing out on something, my days consisting of little but work and sitting in cafeneions. One thing I never lacked was Peter's love so I didn't feel that I had cause to complain.

In the middle of August Peter thought it would make a nice change to go to Corfu for the rest of the summer, from where we could go to Italy in good time for the festivals in Puglia, where we could make a lot of money in a short time. I didn't mind leaving Kefalonia, beautiful though it was, and could hardly wait to stay in the youth hostel for a few days just for the pleasure of a shower and to be able to wash our clothes, our squat being so far from a beach that I hardly ever had time to go swimming and usually just washed myself down with a bottle of water. We worked hard to make the money to get to Corfu and one evening realized the dream of a lifetime when Peter's first customer, a bearded Greek, bought the complete portfolio of pictures! In a heady state of exultation we left Argostoli next day and took the ferry to Patras.

Back at the youth hostel we fell into our old routine, I sitting in the garden to paint more watercolours to sell and Felix spending all day trying unsuccessfully to catch the rabbits that Theodoro had acquired. With our new found wealth Peter spent rather more than he intended on a fruit machine in one of the cafeneions, and after several days of good living we no longer had the money for the tickets to Corfu. Peter airily pooh-poohed my concern since there was no reason why we shouldn't go direct to Italy as usual. What was the problem?

As soon as I'd collected enough pictures we went out together to sell them in the restaurants, but it was so much more difficult to sell to the locals that it wasn't long before the youth hostel bill started to mount up again, Peter being the eternal optimist and always underestimating what we owed. One day he ran into three German truckers whom he'd met once or twice when he'd been with Otto, and when they invited him to join them for an evening of playing pool, he was all too eager for the change from selling pictures. One evening stretched to three, with Peter oblivious to the necessity to do a bit of work. When the truckers left Peter reluctantly went out selling again, and for a few days we broke even again, with the exception of the debit. Then, one Saturday morning I awoke with cystitis and was unable to work. I needed to get antibiotics, and quickly, but as it was the weekend there was only one chemist open and that was crammed with people. I didn't know what the word for cystitis was in Greek so all I could do was to describe my symptoms ('I have to urinate frequently and it *hurts*') and pray that they didn't think I had some unmentionable sexual disease. Everybody in the shop became interested and my malady was discussed by both customers and staff while I stood there, crimson with shame and trying to look as if I didn't care. There was a white-coated man sitting at a table by the door.

'Let me take your blood pressure,' he advised, beckoning me over.

'That's not what I need,' I whimpered, but I was urged forward by well-meaning customers telling me, 'Go on, go on. It's free.'

So I had my blood pressure taken and was pronounced fit, and meanwhile the debate regarding my complaint raged round the shop: 'Could it be . . . no, no . . . I think it's . . . but it sounds like . . .' and so on. All of a sudden a girl behind the counter announced that she knew what was wrong with me and delved into a cabinet for a box of tablets, giving me detailed instructions as to the dosage. I paid up and left, relieved that my ordeal was over and hoping that the diagnosis was correct. In two days I was cured and able to paint again.

And then we had a stroke of luck. One of the restaurant-owners who had seen my paintings wanted some of them reproduced on a mammoth scale on the walls of his restaurant, and asked Peter if he would do the work. Peter was delighted to have this opportunity to do some painting in his own right and negotiated a price. The pictures were selected and I did the sketches for Peter to paint, some of them anyway since two of the murals were to be on walls out of my reach. I have no head for heights so Peter did these himself, balancing on a rickety stepladder with the paintbrush tied to a broom handle. Another problem was that each employee of the restaurant was allowed a say in what he wanted personally and Peter was obliged to make so many changes that the resulting murals looked nothing like the original watercolours that had been ordered. However, at last the mammoth work was completed to everyone's satisfaction and Peter was paid the money without demur. Rich once more, we floated home on cloud nine to pay our bill at the youth hostel and the day after we bought our tickets and caught the ferry to Brindisi.

We arrived at midday and as there seemed to be nobody around in the gardens by the port, we had a beer and went straight to the squat in Casale. The only people there were Helmuth and Wolfgang, who told us that Volker and Mahler Klaus had gone to France, and Lapsi, Bernd and another German were living in a squat nearer to Brindisi. The atmosphere was very much quieter than the last time we'd stayed there, but it didn't last long since Otto arrived the following day.

'Oh, no,' groaned Helmuth, laughing, as Otto put down his rucksack with a hearty shout of greeting. 'I like to see you, Otto, but I like it better when I see you pick *up* your pack and face the other way!'

For the next few days Otto attached himself to Peter, insisting on his company whenever he went begging because it was so much more entertaining, and spending every evening in boisterous reminiscences as we sat round the table playing yahtzee. Fortunately we didn't have to endure his company for long because the festival season had started so Peter and I were able to go off for days at a time, leaving Felix in Helmuth's care.

Our first festival was at Francavilla Fontana and lasted for three days, culminating on Peter's birthday with a firework display even grander than the one we had seen in Bari. Considering that there were several other Madonnaros at work, I had done extremely well with my huge picture on the ground, maybe because I represented the original picture more faithfully than the others, but the towns-folk remembered Peter from previous years, so when he gave two fire-shows each evening, he made almost double the amount of money than I did. We celebrated our birthdays jointly in the squat with a massive array of food and drink, and went to our next festi-val in Copertina with terrible hangovers. After that came Modugno, where I was befriended by two small boys who took me round all the churches in town, and following that we went to Montalbano, Gravina and Ginosa, returning to Brindisi between each festival to relax and recuperate. I needed these periods in which to recover because, although we made a lot of money, I found the festivals were too stressful. Peter was unfazed by all the crowds, but he understood my feelings and helped me all he could.

It was the beginning of October, so we decided to call it a day and go back to Sicily, both of us looking forward to living in our cave once again. We took the train straight through to Siracusa, not wanting to stop even for a few hours in Reggio Calabria, but pausing at Russo's for a wine on the way home from the station. Bernd was there with the dogs but seemed very much less alert than in the past. He told us that Little Lupo had gone to Sardinia and only five of them lived in the cave now – himself, Uwe, Mario, Wolle and Salvatore. Big Lupo had gone back into hospital, but had died six weeks previous to our arrival, such sad news since Peter and I had always liked him and it seemed only a short time ago that he used to come up to our cave and play with Felix.

We were greeted by a tall, bearded Austrian called Eric whom we'd once met in Patras, who was now living in the cave round the corner from Bernd, together with Jurgen, Eyetie Otto and Karina, who'd been trying to persuade one of them to take her to Portugal. We heard that Irish Pete had gone to Rome and that our cave needed a new door, since he'd come home drunk one night and broken it down when he couldn't find the key.

'No problem,' said Peter when we arrived at the cave and inspected the damage, and he hung a new one made simply of a canvas-covered frame with a portion cut out of the top to let in the light. Mario was so pleased to see us back that he came up for three

160

days in succession to cook and eat with us, enthusing about the 'good old days' when there was always a crowd of people up at our cave.

'We don't really want a crowd of people round our cave, Mario,' Peter explained tactfully. 'We moved here to be on our own and, yes, we like to see people from time to time, but not every day. Really we were glad to get away for the summer, it was just too much.'

Being an understanding type, Mario took the hint and we saw less of him, but then Carlo moved into the cave vacated by Irish Pete. His own had been reclaimed by the authorities so he had no choice but to move out, bringing with him his two large dogs, Strollz and Sue, with their two puppies and two cats.

'I'm going to like it here,' he announced, rubbing his hands in anticipation. 'We can play yahtzee in the evenings. Ha, ha, ha.'

Peter and I were glad to have him as a neighbour to begin with, remembering him as a person who enjoyed socializing on occasions, but also liking to keep to himself a lot of the time. Knowing that he wasn't keen on cooking, Peter invited him to eat with us at lunchtime, not realizing that Carlo was a stickler for punctuality and liked to eat no later than two o'clock. All went well to start with, but the first time that we got sidetracked by friends and arrived home an hour later, Carlo informed us huffily that in future he would do his own cooking.

'It's not good enough, Peter,' he said pompously. 'When you have guests it's your duty to be on time.'

'Duty my arse,' said Peter shortly. 'You're welcome to eat with us when we cook, but I don't have to run my life around your mealtimes.'

We soon discovered that it wasn't only meals that he liked on time. Not only was he the only person I'd met on the street who was a teetotaller, but he liked to keep to a strict routine in everything, setting his alarm to go begging at a precise hour and giving his dogs their run also at a particular time. The dogs and cats always had a specific amount of food, grams per kilo according to the free booklet he got from a pet shop, and he bought a pair of scales so that the food could be measured out correctly. His dogs were inoculated annually and were not allowed to have fleas or worms, and for the latter he examined their turds daily. I admired him in a way, but apart from his dismissive attitude to other vagabonds whom he considered less responsible, his topics of conversation were unvaried and yawn-inducing.

'Huh, I made 47,000 lire today,' he'd tell me, throwing himself onto our settee when he got back from work. 'That's not bad for two hour's work, but I spent 31,000 lire at the supermarket and it'll cost me another 5,000 lire to do the football pools. Bari lost again, donner wetter, ha, ha, ha. Dogfood's gone up by 100 lire a tin, so I'm going to put them on dried food. Huh, I'll have to fill up the water canisters again. It takes twenty litres to wash a pullover, you know. Strollz jumped up at me so I'll have to wash my jeans again too, and detergent's expensive . . .' Zzzzzzzzzzzzz.

I spent a lot of time in the cave, painting pictures on canvas for different people, including one for Padre Rufino portraying the martyrdom of Santa Lucia. In the evening, however, I'd always go down to the wine house to join Peter for a drink as he liked to have me beside him. On our way home together we often called in to the club where Signora Rita worked and Beppe, who was intensely curious to see our cave, asked if he might bring a friend round to visit us one evening. Two nights later, as we were playing yahtzee with Carlo and Wolle, we heard shouts of 'permesso' outside and Beppe appeared with a young man who could have passed for Rupert Brooke. I had always found him a bit effeminate, but on this occasion both Beppe and his friend surpassed themselves. Clasping their hands together in ecstasy, they gazed round the cave and pronounced it 'perfectly enchanting'. They sat down next to me on the rickety settee and, giggling and fluttering their eyelashes, they accepted some wine and wanted to learn how to play yahtzee. I showed them and they went into squeals of delight as they threw the dice, jumping up and clapping their hands every time they scored anything, giggling and simpering at the three hairy Germans sitting silently opposite until I found it impossible to keep a straight face myself. They enjoyed themselves so much that they turned up for the next three evenings in succession, full of squeals, giggles and shrieks of delight, until Peter asked Beppe to warn us if he wanted

162

to visit, since we liked to go out on our own sometimes. He needn't have bothered to say anything, in fact, because the visits ceased not long after that when Beppe and most of the family, including the dodgy uncle who ran the club, were jailed for drug-trafficking.

The Santa Lucia festival came, thunderously advertised on the first morning with cannons being fired from just above the cave, sending Felix diving under the duvet with fright. We worked hard for the whole eight days, I making the pictures and Peter collecting, every so often taking it in turns to have a break in the wine house. Then it was time for the Father Christmas tour. The dogs in the big cave had stolen and destroyed Peter's beard, so I made another one out of cotton wool, but although it looked all right at the beginning of each evening, during the course of a few hours with Father Christmas stopping at every bar for a brandy, it became increasingly sodden, limp and horrible to behold and I invariably had to make a new one the next day. Yet however disreputable Father Christmas looked, he continued to remain popular and we were never short of funds for our Christmas treats.

Christmas Day was lovely, slightly quieter than previous years as we were able to spend more time on our own, but New Year's Eve was as sociable as ever. Some Germans had arrived from Reggio Calabria, and Salvatore brought home a group of English and Italian people to stay in the cave. The two English girls were both called Amanda and both from Fleet where I'd lived with my grandparents as a child, and their friend was Jamie, a quick-witted character with dreadlocks and eyes almost as blue as Peter's. They were young, lively and full of fun, and we greeted 1993 with a resounding chorus of 'Auld Lang Syne', as we set off fireworks and drank quantities of sparkling wine on a night as clear and starry as the first I'd seen in the cave. I'd been with Peter for three years and I was as much in love with him as ever.

14 The Old Boat

I loved the springtime in Siracusa, bringing with it a vast blue carpet of wild irises that bloomed beyond the alyssum and lady's-slipper in the cactus ring. I don't think that Peter was quite as entranced as I was by the beauty of the place, being rather more prosaic and appreciative of the practicalities of our position on the hillside and the fact that we were so close to the centre of town and the wine houses. We had discovered a new one very much closer to the cave than either Russo's or the Cornuto, and had taken to drinking there. It was only a tiny place and run by a forthright character called Natale who argued and shouted as loudly as his clients. A lot of the local fishermen gathered there as well as the manual labourers and I loved the noisy atmosphere, the joking and laughter and the fact that I was included in the conversation even if a lot of it went over my head. Some of the men spoke in a strong Sicilian dialect, particularly Santo, who talked loudly, rapidly and at great length to me in his harsh staccato voice that sounded like machine-gun fire. I merely sat there smiling, looking interested and saying 'yes' or 'no' at intervals, which made everybody laugh as they all knew I could understand hardly a word.

Peter's Sicilian friends came round with increasing frequency to our cave, usually after the wine houses closed for lunch, so that we could all continue our discussion where we had left off. One of the many Pippos in Siracusa, Pippo Tedesco, brought round a large octopus for lunch one day. He was a sweet man whom I rarely saw sober, and the only person that I ever met who could

165

remain standing while leaning either backwards or forwards at an angle of almost forty-five degrees. On this occasion he allowed Peter to do the pasta but wanted to cook the octopus himself.

'It's such a delicacy, my favourite food,' he told us, caressing it almost lovingly as he dropped it into the boiling water, then sat

166

down with a glass of wine while it bubbled away. When the pasta was ready Pippo hoicked out the octopus and plopped it heavily onto the biggest dish we had, where it sat staring at us, all glistening, brown and octopussy, its arms dangling over the edge of the plate. My appetite receded as Pippo cut off bits of arm to put on our plates, but though I couldn't face the skin or the suckers, I chewed away manfully at the white flesh which tasted like crab but had the texture of rubber. Peter told me afterwards that it hadn't been cooked nearly long enough.

'Have a piece of the head, that's the best bit,' said Pippo, smacking his lips as he sliced it open and all the dark brown liquid spewed out. 'The juice makes a *delicious* sauce for the pasta,' and he slurped it onto his plate with gusto. Peter refused it but I tried some and I'm afraid it didn't make *my* taste buds blossom, so after plying Pippo with more wine, we put the remains of the octopus into a plastic bag, the viscous liquid into a jar, and gave it all to him to take home.

At that time my opinion of Sicilian cooking was rather low, having had a worse experience only a few weeks earlier. A Sicilian girl, Raphaella, and her husband used to visit us from time to time and she had cooked a meal for us on a couple of occasions, the first one pasta with some invisible sauce, the second one, snails. I'd never tried snails but Peter loved them and was looking forward to the meal; but unfortunately Raphaella, like Pippo, cooked them for far too short a time and they were so raw that they almost crawled out of their shells unassisted, their horns still protruding accusingly. I managed to swallow three and Peter gagged after the first, yet Raphaella and her husband devoured the rest with evident relish. Fortunately we discovered later that neither of these meals were representative of Sicilian cuisine.

Bruno, a fisherman friend, quite often brought us plastic boxes or jars full of all sorts of delicacies that he or his wife had made, mostly fish cooked in the most delectable sauces. I tried snails again, cooked by a Signora Lucia, and although they looked unattractive, coming out of their shells like little black corkscrews and rather chewy, their flavour, cooked with onions and tomatoes, was lovely. As for a meal we had with Gino Dattaglia, that was some-thing never to be forgotten, the pasta sauce so rich and thick with eggs, cream, mushrooms, peas and tomatoes, that the pasta itself almost disappeared, and his homemade wine was the best I'd ever tasted.

In addition to being an excellent cook Gino was also a hard drinker, and one day after the wine house closed, he and a friend stopped by at our cave to continue the drinking session. Many wines later he decided to go home but found that he was in no condition to drive his motorbike and accepted a lift with a friend, asking Peter to deliver the bike to the wine house, from where he would collect it that evening. Peter had no problem driving it down but Gino never turned up, however, so we had to take it home again, first stopping for a few wines and a laugh with the people in the big cave. Peter then decided that the night was young and he would go round to Pippo Tedesco to watch football on the tele-vision but on leaving the cave he drove straight into the path of a car. The bike was severely mangled, his ring finger only slightly less so, and as it was still bleeding and mutilated the following morning, I persuaded him to go to the hospital.

The doctor told him that there was no alternative but for the finger to be amputated immediately so Peter and I walked along to the operating theatre and sat dutifully outside while other patients in varying degrees of disability went in and out. Every so often a head would pop out to tell Peter to wait five minutes and they'd deal with him, but four hours later we were still there and the surgeon and his entourage came out smoking cigarettes and telling us to come back after lunch. Peter had had enough, however, and stalked out furiously saying that he would cure his finger himself. We headed straight for Natale's wine house for some much needed refreshment and Pippo Bravo gave us a lift home. He told us that the flesh of cactus was ideal for healing wounds and peeled a slice to encase Peter's finger under the bandage I'd prepared from a torn sheet. The final outcome was that the finger healed up completely and although it remained inert, at least Peter's hand looked normal.

When Gino heard about the accident he hurried round to make sure that Peter was all right, caring little for the damage to his bike. He turned up at the cave the following morning with two bottles of his exquisite homemade wine and two live hens in a sack. I tried

to explain that we couldn't possibly keep the hens because we'd be leaving for Greece in a month or so but Gino said we'd have to eat them in that case because he'd stolen them and had no use for them himself.

So the hens stayed, Madam Frankenstein and Anna. Peter built them a little enclosure for the night-time and they roamed free during the day, scratching around in the cactus ring or, more often, lurking by the cave entrance, hopping in when nobody was looking and gobbling up whatever remained in Felix's bowl. They refused the chicken meal that Peter bought for them and thrived on what was left over from our meals. Madam Frankenstein, the older hen, became fat and lazy and ceased to lay eggs after the first few weeks, giving herself dust baths in the sun and complaining loudly all day. Anna was more obliging and laid an egg a day until we left. Felix, who'd given birth to kittens a few weeks before the hens appeared, was fascinated by them, especially the fat Madam Frankenstein who once seized a lizard from her and gobbled it down before she knew what had happened.

Some new people arrived in Siracusa and moved into the cave with Jurgen and Eyetie Otto, Eric and Karina having left to go to Austria. There were two youngish East Germans, Gerhardt and Kurt, who were new to the vagabond life, an elderly Swiss called Peter and a grey-haired, grey-bearded German with a dog – Lobo and Lobby respectively. They were such good company that Peter and I visited them quite often, Lobo especially interesting as he'd travelled a lot and done so many different things. He was a writer, was fluent in Spanish and had a beautiful singing voice too, a rich baritone which he loved to exercise whenever Jurgen played his guitar.

Manny suddenly returned to Siracusa, but so different from the loveable hamster I remembered that I didn't recognize him at first. His manner was vague and he had lost a lot of weight, as well as all his teeth, looking like a little old man and unable to drink without lapsing into unconsciousness. He, Jurgen, the two East Germans and Eyetie Otto (who'd also gone very much to seed over the past year) moved into the apartment where Peter and I had once stayed, though they were sensible enough to go to the local

170

council and obtain official authority first. Peter and I went round to a party there, but we couldn't help thinking complacently how lucky we were to have moved out, as it looked so dull and uninspiring in comparison to our beautiful cave.

By the end of May spring was turning into summer, and one could hear the wild peas popping in the surrounding undergrowth as one attended to the calls of nature. We needed to make the money to go to Greece again and in addition to working on the pavement, I painted watercolours for Peter to hawk round the shops in town as well as embarking on the odd picture in acrylic on canvas, mostly portraits and pictures of saints. Gaetano, one of the regulars in Russo's wine house, brought me some models of Sicilian carts that he'd made and asked me to paint traditional Sicilian designs on them. It was work that I thoroughly enjoyed as the designs were so colourful and different from what I normally painted, although the old rogue paid me only a third of what we'd agreed. I have to say that Gaetano wasn't the only one to short-change us as several unscrupulous people took advantage of the fact that, because we were so short of money, we would accept a deposit to secure the picture on the promise of the balance later yet full payment did not necessarily materialize and occasionally we would be forced to beg in order to survive.

Luckily we got a lot of help from our Sicilian friends. Padre Rufino and his colleague, Padre Giacomo, regularly gave us plastic bags full of the staple foods, Agostino and his father gave us as many oranges and lemons as we needed and Mauritsio gave us vegetables for a fraction of the normal price. Bruno gave us fish that he'd caught as well as jars of his pickled olives, chillies and dried tomatoes which spiced up the simplest of meals. All sorts of herbs grew in the terrain around our cave as well as wild asparagus and prickly pears and, had I been really keen, I would have collected snails to cook and eat, but after Raphaella's offering I was never tempted to do that. Clothes, of course, were never a problem as we were given so many, and there were other ways in which we made small savings. The white chalk that I used for my pavement pictures made a good substitute for toothpaste and washing-up liquid cleaned everything from clothes to ourselves as well as being a good retarder for the acrylic paints that I used. I also discovered that the soda used by the men to settle their stomachs made a good tooth-whitener as well as a de-stinker of shoes and though I couldn't afford hair dye, being rather vain I covered the grey bits with a mixture of red and green Indian ink that I'd been given, which produced a curious shade of brown and amused laughter from Peter.

Eventually we saved enough money to take us all the way to Greece. We'd found homes for Felix's kittens and we took her with us, giving the chickens to a delighted Carlo, who'd been calculating how much money he could save if he bought some for himself. We bought our tickets to Brindisi, arriving the following morning and taking the bus to Casale to find that Lapsi, Bernd and Volker were still away and only Helmuth and Wolfgang remained. The atmosphere was somewhat strained with Helmuth glued silently to his television all day, while Wolfgang seemed to do most of the household chores, limping back and forth with a martyred expression on his face and his habitual sniff. We decided not to linger and took the ferry to Patras.

Knowing our limitations where paying off the youth hostel bill was concerned, we headed straight for Kefalonia, only to find our building site of the previous year in Argostoli was being worked on. Once again Felix and I were left with the rucksacks outside a cafeneion while Peter searched for somewhere else to sleep. He found a very old wooden boat on the seashore opposite the gypsy camp, virtually rotted away but with a fairly sound platform on which to sleep and with adequate shelter from the elements once Peter had found some plastic sheeting to drape over the top. As before, I painted in the back of the brothers' cafeneion and we ate in the same cheap restaurant, but every evening when we returned home for the night we found that the rucksack had been emptied out and one or two insignificant items taken – a tin of catfood, a mirror and that sort of thing. Peter complained to the chief of the gypsy camp and was told that it must have been Albanians who'd done the thieving but the following afternoon I

172

stayed in the boat instead of going to the cafeneion as usual and, as dusk was falling, I surprised a gypsy girl climbing in. I shouted after her retreating back that I'd call the police, and told Peter what had happened. I don't think that we would have had any more trouble after that, but Peter was angry that his complaint to the gypsy chief had gone unheeded and after registering his second complaint, just to show that he was aware of what went on, he went in search of a better place to live. He found it, somewhere almost as nice as our cave. It was an old caique with a carved figurehead, propped up on wooden blocks in the boatyard at the other end of the town, and when Peter asked the yard's manager, Spiro, if we could live on it for a while, he was told that there would be no objection at all since the boat would never be fit to go to sea again.

So we moved in immediately, and it was like heaven after the buildng site and the rotten boat. We slept in the pointed end and cooked on the shelf above the instrument panel on a camping-gas cooker that we bought, and though it was rather noisy during the day because of the bulldozers working on the new marina, I was able to do my painting there and enjoyed the company of Felix. Being made of wood, the boat got incredibly hot and I felt as if I was working in a sauna, the sweat pouring off me in rivulets all day, but I took a masochistic pleasure in the thought that it was doing me good and it was so refreshing to be able to climb down the

173

ladder and cool off in the sea whenever I wanted. Peter's selling technique improved to the extent that he could afford to hire a little motorbike, which meant that he could sell further afield than before, as well as taking me for trips to other parts of the island so that I could have a break from painting. I needed to paint a minimum of six pictures a day for Peter to sell in order to keep us in the style to which we were rapidly becoming accustomed, so if I worked hard and painted at least one extra watercolour a day, once a week I could have a day off. At least, that was the theory, but in practice I often didn't meet my official target, so any extra pictures I could produce went towards that and I got a day off far less frequently than Peter had predicted. Sometimes I'd get exasperated because my painting wasn't coming as it should and the heat was so extreme, and I'd feel sorry for myself and aggrieved that Peter was sitting in a cafeneion all day playing cards, while I was having to work long hours in temperatures of over ninety degrees. Then I would come to my senses and realize that despite the discomforts, it was my choice, I was doing something that I enjoyed, nobody was pushing me except myself, and I was with a man whom I adored and who adored me.

I was told that the weather was particularly extreme that year, 1993, and even in the evening it remained hot and airless when I walked into town with my pictures to meet Peter. It was slightly cooler in the cafeneions because of the marble floors and high ceilings, but there was never a breath of wind. Stavros, who had a cafeneion on the seafront near the town centre where I used to sit when Peter was selling on his own, told me lugubriously, 'They're predicting another severe earthquake, I'm afraid. It's exactly forty years since the last 'quake in 1953 when so much of the island was destroyed, and the conditions are the same. I remember it well, as hot as this with no air. Mark my words, the signs are bad.' I was half-dreading, half-thrilled by the prospect of a potential adventure, but fortunately the predictions were wrong and the summer passed with only a minor earth tremor.

I had started doing portraits in the evening, sitting in the main square, the same sort of thing that I'd done when I was in Corinth with Peter and Otto, only not so much fun because my clientele was so different and both I and my customers in Argostoli were always

174

sober. I made better money with the portraits than with the water-colours, but the light wasn't good and, being very short-sighted, I had problems seeing well enough to sketch, although I got round it to a large extent by wearing only one contact lens so that I could see my subject through that, and see my paper with the bad eye. The portrait venture was brought to a close early, however, when I was savaged by a dog.

The animal had been left tied to the railings outside the boatyard in the hot sun, without water, shade or food, and its distressed whimpering prompted me to give it water throughout the day. When dusk began to fall and it was time to meet Peter in town, I gave it a bowl of leftover scraps from our lunch, but made the mistake of reaching for the waterbowl to refill that, at the same time. As was to be expected, I suppose, the dog grabbed my arm savagely and blood started to spurt all over the place, but my main worry was my precious watercolours, which I held out at a distance as I hurried, rather shakily, over to the yard for help. Giving me a plastic bag to bleed into, Spiro and his friend drove me at speed to the hospital, where I was given swift and effective treatment. After being doused and scrubbed with neat alcohol, iodine was poured liberally over my wounds and an antibiotic spray applied before I was bandaged up. Astonishingly there was no anti-tetanus vaccine in the hospital and I had to telephone Peter at the cafeneion and ask him to buy some and deliver it so that I could be injected. Luckily, although my hand was very stiff next day, I could still use it to paint my watercolours after a fashion, but I was too slow and unsure of myself to attempt the portraits and went thankfully back to doing my crosswords or reading in the cafeneion while Peter did his selling.

Then the weather changed, the rain came down and our boat leaked so that on a couple of nights we had to take our sleeping bags and doss down in the shelter of a building site nearby. We weren't able to leave until the beginning of October because Felix had given birth to a couple of kittens and we had to wait until they were old enough to go to the homes we'd found for them. However, at last we were free and said goodbye to Kefalonia for another year.

15   Siracusan Anecdotes

The journey as far as Brindisi went without a hitch, Felix settling down on the ferry like a seasoned traveller, but the main journey from there to Reggio Calabria was miserable, Felix refusing to stay calm and wailing plaintively all night long to Peter's great distress. We stayed with Thomas in his luxury squat which now had running water, electricity and a colour television. He also had a canary in which Felix took a most unseemly interest, so much so that Peter and I were obliged to take her into the park and leave her to chase pigeons while we were at work in the morning. We needed the money for the last leg of our journey so Peter begged while I went round the shops to sell the remainder of my watercolours and in two days we were able to buy our tickets for Siracusa.

It was lovely to find our cave as we'd left it although the surrounding terrain, with the exception of the trees and the cactus ring, was brown, dry and devoid of flowers, the summer having been even hotter in Sicily than in Greece. No sooner had we arrived than Carlo lumbered in and sat on the chest with a crash, tripping up and sending the empty water canisters flying as he did so. With shouts of laughter he told us that Jurgen and Eyetie Otto had been evicted from the apartment for stealing electricity and were now living with Lobo and Swiss Peter in the cave round the corner from Bernd. One of the English girls had left but Jamie and the other one were still in the big cave together with Uwe, who'd been in hospital for most of the summer with ulcerous feet, and Salvatore, who was causing more trouble than ever. On the home front, he'd eaten Madame Frankenstein shortly after we'd left because she'd stopped laying eggs, and Strollz had killed and eaten Anna and got a thrashing for it.

It felt good to go down to Natale's wine house that evening and meet up with all our friends again and catch up with all the summer's gossip. Amanda and Jamie turned up and so did Bernd and Uwe, who told me that he'd lost all feeling in his feet but since they weren't painful any more he didn't intend to go back to the hospital. I thought he was crazy to ignore something like that but he giggled whimsically and told me in his southern drawl that as long as he slept well, had friends around him and was healthy enough to go begging he wasn't going to spoil things. He seemed quite unperturbed but Jamie told me later that he wasn't so easy-going in the cave, drinking more than ever and quarrelling with everybody. I never saw that side of him, I'm happy to say, and was glad that Peter and I were away from all the bickering and strife.

We were beginning to wish Carlo didn't live so close because he seemed to spend more time in our cave than in his own. When he finished work he invariably called in to chat to me about all his domestic trivia while I painted, and after going back to his cave to do his chores he'd turn up again at lunchtime and talk endlessly to Peter about football, his other passion, and would only leave when Peter got into bed to have a siesta. As soon as we got back from the wine house in the evenings, Carlo would reappear at the door with a loud greeting and clutching his bottle of Fanta, all ready for a game of cards. We'd taken to playing rummy and Carlo preferred that because he played to win and, unfortunately, usually did, rubbing his hands together in triumph and shouting 'hah!' as he slammed down the winning hand. It was most annoying.

When Gaetano found out that we were back in Siracusa, he hung around outside Russo's wine house until he managed to bump into Peter and ask him, all smiles, if I'd paint some more Sicilian carts for him. Clearly he felt that enough months had passed for the money he owed us to be regarded as water under the bridge, but Peter told him that any more work he wanted done would have to be paid for in advance.

'But Peter, dear boy,' he pleaded, 'you know that I don't get the money for the carts until they're sold. I'm completely broke at the moment but I'll pay you as soon as the work's done.'

'Sorry, Gaetano,' Peter said implacably, 'but no money, no work. We have to live too.'

Finally, after several weeks, the old rascal produced the cash and I painted the carts for him. I was given several orders for my pictures of saints on canvas, which was just as well because the weather became cold and wet and I was lucky not to have to rely on my pavement art. Our cave leaked and we had to collect all the drips in a number of pots and pans which Carlo never failed to trip over when he charged in for his evening game of cards. He was incapable of doing anything gently and, apart from slopping rainwater everywhere and laughing uproariously as he did so, it wasn't long before our settee collapsed under him and we had to prop it up on rocks.

The weather cleared for the Santa Lucia festival and, as usual, we woke to the thunder of cannon-fire and the smell of cordite as the cave shuddered under the heavy guns. We worked up at the Dome on the first day and thereafter outside Padre Rufino's church. Giacomo, the beggar, wasn't there so we made a handsome collection every day, as well as selling each of the pictures as I finished them. No sooner had the festival ended than Peter made his, by now obligatory, Father Christmas tour of the town, being frequently called upon to appear at people's houses to distribute gifts to children. Irish Pete arrived for Christmas in the company of a German we knew from Catania, and a few days later all the cave-dwellers were invited to a dinner organized by the Church of Santa Lucia for the people of the parish. We were seated at random amongst Sicilian families and as there was no shortage of alcohol nobody felt in the least inhibited. After the gargantuan meal someone sat down at the piano and played a medley of Sicilian and Italian folk songs, with everybody joining in to sing, and that was followed by dancing, Padre Ruffino and Padre Giacomo whirling around amongst the dancers with their cassocks flying. We may

179

have looked shabby and unkempt in comparison to the locals but we were made to feel not only welcome but accepted, and it was a thoroughly contented group of people who wended our way home to the caves that night.

Early in the New Year I went to England. It was lovely to stay with my mother and to see my family again and I wallowed in the luxury of hot baths and central heating, but I found the constant hurrying to and fro in pursuit of one thing or another too weary-ing for my taste, and I missed Peter and the simplicity of life in the cave and was glad when the time came to fly back.

Peter met me at Palermo, his face creased into a welcoming grin. Confused about the date I was to return, he had been lurking around the airport for the last two days and had been befriended by two airport policemen who had allowed him to doss down in their office because they hadn't liked the idea of his sleeping out in the cold. He'd told them about me so I had to meet them and show them my pictures, although we declined their offer to sleep in the terminal building and took the last train out of Palermo, ending up in Cefalu. We found a bar to spend the rest of the evening in, delighting in each other's company, and then it was time to search for a sleeping place and collect some cardboard boxes. Peter heaved me up and over a wall, on the other side of which was a building site where we flattened out the cardboard boxes and bedded down for the night. It was warm even though it was only mid-February and we slept blissfully until next morning when we were awakened by the workers.

We arrived in Siracusa at lunchtime and met Bernd and Wolle with the dogs outside Russo's wine house. We stopped for a wine and were quite shocked by what we heard – Lobo had died on the way to hospital only two nights ago. I'd always thought Lobo to be one of the more healthy of the cavemen, since he looked well, ate well and was always interesting company, but Peter told me that he drank a phenomenal amount of wine. I'd never noticed. Swiss Peter had taken Lobby (Lobo's dog) and moved out of town and their cave was now empty. There was also a card from Lupo to say that he was in hospital in Cagliari with lung problems but that he hoped to be back in the summer.

180

Carlo took to spending even more time with us than before and had taken to chaining his bitch, Sue, outside our cave when he went to work in the morning because she was on heat. It seemed a bit of a liberty but we wouldn't have minded if it hadn't been for her continuous and hysterical barking. However, after three weeks had passed and Sue was still with us in the morning, Peter asked Carlo why he couldn't leave her with the other dogs as she clearly missed their company.

'There isn't enough space outside my cave,' Carlo told us impatiently. 'Anyway, it's only for a couple of hours a day. Surely you can put up with her for that long.'

It appeared that we had no choice, and we did our best to close our ears to the barking, though it affected me more than Peter as he simply escaped to the wine house after breakfast. We felt sorry for her too, and got into the habit of giving her the odd titbit which always quietened her temporarily. Early one Sunday morning, however, when we usually had some peace, Carlo came stomping round with Sue to chain her up, clearly in a rage about something and shouting that she was not to be given any treats. Peter had already gone out and I have never been a bundle of laughs at that time of day, so Carlo's manner was like a red rag to a bull.

'How *dare* you tell me what I can or cannot do outside *my* cave!' I hissed furiously. 'I'm *sick* of Sue's barking! She gives me a headache so that I can't work and I've had just about enough, and if you leave her I shall set her free! There!'

This unexpected outburst from a mere woman sent Carlo into even more of a passion and, his eyes glittering, almost foaming at the mouth, he dragged Sue off with him, snarling that if a mere couple of hours barking gave me a headache, he'd ensure that he kept all his dogs tied up throughout the whole day and then I really would have a headache. Moreover, he would NEVER set foot in our cave again. I told Peter what had happened and he grinned 'Better so, Baby-Prue'. Carlo was prone to the sulks and had often fallen out with us before over some imagined slight and stayed away for a day or so, but this time he was obviously serious and kept his word. It was wonderful, like those first few weeks in our cave when

181

life had been so tranquil, and we relished having the place to ourselves again. Another happy side effect was that Carlo didn't, in fact, keep his dogs chained up all day, but set them free whenever he was home, so they benefited too.

March came in and the sun came out and the whole area became a feast of wild flowers, the cactus sprouting myriads of yellow blossoms, with countless others carpeting the ground in patches of pink, blue, yellow and white. I got so much pleasure out of the nature that surrounded us, the birds and the butterflies, the scent of herbs and of honey, and day after day of clear, blue skies. In the warmth of the springtime I went into town every day to work on the pavement with renewed enthusiasm, both morning and evening, Peter collecting for me occasionally but more often on my own. I usually met him in the wine house afterwards but one day he'd twisted his ankle climbing over the rocks and stayed at home, so after work I went straight back to the cave. Just as I was taking a short cut through the blocks of flats, a motorbike passed dangerously close to me and I could feel a tugging at my shoulder. My mind was on other things so I wasn't really concentrating and assumed that the handlebars of the bike had got entangled with my workbag and let go of everything to avoid an accident. Alas, I realized too late that I had been mugged, my bag had been grabbed by the pillion rider and I watched, dumbfounded, as they vanished round a corner. I wasn't hurt but I wasn't happy since, in addition to all my coloured chalks and a few watercolours, I'd lost a canvas portrait that I'd done of Peter. My only consolation was that I must have looked well dressed enough to be considered worth mugging in the first place.

The Cornuto wine house had closed down in December but in March it reopened under new ownership, that of the innovative Mario Biondo and his wife Lucia. It was unrecognizable from the dark and dingy establishment that it had been before, as Mario had completely redecorated it and opened up a room at the back with tables and chairs so that people could sit and drink in comfort, talking or playing cards as they wished. Peter, in half an hour of drunken zeal, did a cartoon in chalk of dogs drinking at the bar and presented it to Mario on the opening night. All of us from the caves were invited to the party and, with the exceptions of Signora Lucia, Amanda and myself, the place was thronged with men, including most of the clientele from the other wine houses. There was an almost old-fashioned air of gaiety with all the joking and laughter, the singing of the traditional Sicilian and Neapolitan songs, the drumming on the tables to the rhythm of the tambourines and the general atmosphere of sheer enjoyment of life.

From then on, Mario's became one of our regular drinking places. We still went to Natale's, where I felt very much at home, but Mario stayed open later, so our evenings usually ended up in there and we would sit round a table drinking wine and eating the cheap titbits, including snails, that Signora Lucia provided to absorb the alcohol. It was a slightly more up-market establishment than the other wine houses and, in addition to the regulars, I often noticed rather more influential-looking characters drinking there. Peter said that a lot of them had been in jail, like himself, and although I thought he was exaggerating, when I looked around I realized that he was probably right. I knew personally, and disliked, at least two drugs dealers and one killer (a family vendetta) who'd done time but there were others, friends, whose conversations, when I thought about it, definitely revealed an inside knowledge of the penitentiary system. Peter had often pointed out men who didn't work or have any obvious means of support and yet who had an amazingly lavish lifestyle, but I'd never really contemplated the significance. All I knew was that these people didn't bother us and common sense decreed that we didn't bother about them.

Peter enjoyed playing cards with his Sicilian friend and whenever he got inveigled into a game I sat and gossiped with Irish Pete and Uwe while they painstakingly constructed the little models out of chocolate Kinder eggs. Bernd and Wolle came in occasionally because Bernd liked to be able to sit, but I got the impression that Wolle found Mario's a bit too classy for his taste. There was a certain amount of friction in the cave again, sometimes involving Salvatore but caused a lot of the time by Uwe, whose health problems made him very irascible. Wolle was normally such a quiet and easy-going character, but one evening he sat opposite me in

183

Mario's looking positively ferocious, with narrowed eyes and bared teeth as he told me that 'the peoples' had been stealing his beer. He threatened to set fire to Uwe once and although Uwe escaped his wrath, we did hear that Wolle set fire to someone's sleeping bag after an argument. Fortunately it was empty at the time. A few evenings after that he fell into the harbour and had to be rescued, hotly denying that he was drunk and insisting that he'd been pushed as he tried to save Goliath who'd also fallen in.

Easter was approaching and it became time to think about going to Greece for the summer. I had thought up a new scheme which I was certain would be a good money-spinner and would cost practically nothing as well as being simple though, admittedly, a trifle time-consuming. I made beads out of rolled up pieces of coloured paper, cut from old magazines and, after varnishing them, I made necklaces, bracelets and masses of earrings. They looked extremely pretty and because they were handmade, with every bead unique, Peter and I were both convinced that we could sell them for large sums of money since they were just the sort of thing that no trendy young person could resist. The young people *did* like the beads but, unfortunately, found them very easy to resist at the prices we were charging, so in the end we had to sell them for so little money that they became totally unprofitable. Alas, like the Egg Project and the Yo-yo Project before it, the Bead Project also failed miserably.

Peter and I were always thinking up money-making schemes, some sure-fire way of making our fortune. When he'd been in the Foreign Legion, Peter had been one of their top marksmen, and one of his ideas was to buy two crossbows and re-enact the William Tell story. The plan was that he would fix one crossbow to a rigid structure (unspecified), sighted to point at the target (my job was to check the sights), he would sit on a chair a number of metres distant with the apple on his head, and with the second crossbow he would fire at the trigger mechanism of the first so that the second arrow split the apple. This would all be done to the music of the William Tell Overture and fame and fortune would result. I'm glad to say that we never had enough money to buy the two crossbows that he had in mind, though Peter did buy a cheap one which didn't work properly and which he later sold. On another occasion he wanted to buy a baby crocodile to work with as he'd done in a circus, breezily discounting my objections with regard to travel, Felix, food and so on. Fortunately we didn't have the money and the shopkeeper wisely refused to agree to a hire-purchase proposal.

I went back to my painting and accumulated a number of religious pictures which Peter sold during the Easter period and, in addition to my work on the pavement, by the end of May we had accumulated enough money for our journey to Brindisi. It came as a surprise, earning everyone's eternal gratitude, when Salvatore seriously upset some Sicilians and was ordered to remove himself from Siracusa if he wanted to remain alive. It was no idle threat because the following day some armed Sicilians turned up at the cave to check that he had indeed left. There were fewer people to benefit from the new tranquillity in the cave, however, as Jamie and Amanda had left to go to Sardinia while Irish Pete and Uwe had departed for Catanzaro, but at least the ban ensured a rosier future.

In May, Austrian Eric came back to Siracusa and moved into the cave where Lobo had lived. He got very friendly with Peter and always had his lunch with us, usually because he never had any money. He was a pleasant man who hated begging and wanted to make his living as a tattoo artist, but as most of his clients were wine house regulars with very little money themselves, business was rather infrequent and he was almost always broke. He borrowed from everyone, including Peter and me, but there was always the promise of future business and he liked Siracusa and decided to stay for the summer. We offered him the use of our cave, in which he always did his tattoos anyway, on condition that he would feed Felix for us whenever she appeared (she'd taken to wandering off for days at a time) and he accepted with alacrity. Then Peter heard through the vagabond grapevine that Otto was in hospital in Brindisi and decided to leave Siracusa right away to visit him.

I still had a number of orders for pictures for various people but I didn't mind staying on my own in the cave. I had no qualms about being alone, apart from which we still had two kittens to find homes for, so I was perfectly agreeable to meeting him in the squat in

Casale in a week or so. Although I naturally never considered Peter as an intrusion, loving him as passionately as I did, I enjoyed having the cave to myself and luckily I was usually spared the presence of Eric as he'd taken to spending a lot of his time with Carlo. I took my way of life very much for granted, and it was only one evening as I sat in the cave playing patience by candlelight and pondering to myself, that it suddenly struck me how bizarre it must all seem to people who'd known me five years ago.

'Can this be me or am I dreaming?' I wondered. 'Am I really that same middle-aged woman? Can *I* be talking a mixture of languages and feeling so at home in the company of beggars and alcoholics? Why am I so content, so *happy*, to be living in a cave – or even on the street? But I am, I truly am. I *love* this life.'

On deliberation I realized that I'd never got as much pleasure from living in a house as from living in our cave and feeling so close to nature, although, I reflected, without Peter as my linchpin I might feel differently. I was glad when he telephoned Natale one evening, leaving a message that he was waiting for me and ready to go to Greece, and I couldn't help being amused by his assumption that naturally I would be ready to go too. In fact I had finished the pictures (and been paid) but I still hadn't found homes for the kittens and, on the spur of the moment, I decided to take them with me, not wanting to foist two extra mouths to feed on Eric, who seemed singularly incapable of making money even for himself. So I popped them into a plastic shopping basket as I was leaving and, one being ginger and the other black and white, I unimaginatively named them Orlando and Domino.

Peter met me at Brindisi station and burst into laughter when he saw my guilty expression and my burden. He told me that by the time he'd arrived in Brindisi, Otto had already been discharged from hospital and was back in Germany, so Peter had gone to Lecce and by begging hard he had made the money for the ferry tickets. He wanted to leave that evening so, instead of going to Casale, we bought some wine and pizza and spent the afternoon in the gardens by the port, letting the kittens out to play until it was time to board the ferry.

186

16   Cats, Caves and Carlo

We didn't stay long in Patras as Peter was anxious not to fall into our usual trap of running up a bill at the youth hostel and struggling to pay it off when we could be doing well in Kefalonia. We'd often talked about sleeping rough while we were there but there was something about the youth hostel that always drew us back – the family atmosphere perhaps, and the fact that Theodoro and Dana were always so welcoming. A few days after our arrival, once Peter had reacquainted himself with all his wine house friends, he went on ahead to Kefalonia to make sure that the boat was still there and if he didn't telephone me to the contrary, I was to follow.

There was no telephone call, so two days later I took the ferry to Sami and went from there to Argostoli with Orlando and Domino bobbing about in the shopping bag and causing no problems whatsoever. Peter met me at the bus station and we took a taxi to the boatyard, where I saw that our boat had been moved from its original position over the water to the other side of the road. Inside, everything was just as we'd left it. We put out food and water for the kittens and left them to explore their new home while we walked back into town so that Peter took me on a round of all his favourite cafeneions and pubs.

We speedily got back into our standard routine, I painting pictures during the day and Peter selling them in the evening. I enjoyed life even more than I had done the previous year. The kittens gave us hours of amusement, me in particular as I spent so much time on the boat, and they regularly followed me down to the

187

water whenever I went swimming or came as far as the main road when I went to meet Peter in the evening. The seaboard on the way into town was thick with mussels that year and Peter often collected a bagful for his pasta speciality. There were masses of sea urchins too, but they were more of a bother to prepare, although he'd sometimes collect a few and we'd sit on the sea wall, cutting them open with nail scissors and scooping out the insides with fresh

188

bread. Once again we could afford to hire a motorbike and Peter would take me out to different beaches for a change of scene, and almost every evening he would drive out a few kilometres to the tourist resort of Lassi, which was a lucrative area for selling the pictures. After the strictures of the winter months it was lovely to be affluent again. When neither of us felt like cooking at lunchtime, we would simply wander down to a fish restaurant a hundred metres further along the beach, and if we felt peckish in the evening, which I frequently did, we thought nothing of eating out in a taverna.

The summer drifted luxuriously on until one afternoon Stavro brought over a letter for Peter which, to our surprise, came from Carlo. He reported that he'd been befriended by Austrian Eric but a few weeks before writing, while Carlo had been at work, Eric had gone into his cave and stolen all his savings plus his camera. Needless to say, he had left Siracusa by the time that Carlo had discovered his loss. Carlo also added, with a hint of martyrdom, that Eric had never bothered to feed Felix and that he had been doing so himself whenever she had appeared, but that he hadn't seen her for six weeks and feared that she must have been killed. Peter wanted to go back to Siracusa without delay in case someone else occupied our cave and, as it was the beginning of October, I had a sudden yearning to be back in Siracusa too.

Peter went on ahead but I wanted to give the cats a break and stayed overnight in Brindisi. Wolfgang was no longer in Casale, but there were three other people living in the squat with Helmuth: Stefan, Karl and Oscar. Stefan was a big and amiable, but exceedingly strange lad, Karl looked and acted almost exactly like Otto, and my favourite, Oscar, was a rotund and smiling little Austrian with bushy grey eyebrows and a speech impediment causing him to shout 'ha!' every so often in the course of conversation, which terrified Orlando so that he fled into the trees. I went into town next morning to buy some food for myself and the cats and saw Karl on the same bus on the way back. He was completely drunk, playing his recorder and singing raucously to the other passengers around him, but he didn't see me until we got off the bus together in Casale, whereupon he greeted me joyfully and dropped the huge

189

plastic sackful of butcher's scraps that he was carrying, scattering the contents everywhere. It was a busy main road so as we were picking up all the bits of meat and bones and putting them back into the bag, cars were having to drive onto the verges on either side in order to avoid us. A police car stopped and we were offered assistance, but Karl waved them on in a lordly fashion and we finished the job, staggering home with our load, pieces of meat falling out here and there as we walked and Karl singing loudly all the way.

I left that evening with the cats settled comfortably in their homemade basket, having had to dose Orlando with Helmuth's valium to calm him down. The train journey to Siracusa went smoothly enough, but I was glad to get home to the cave, hugging Peter tightly as I gazed round with delight and saw all our familiar bits and pieces just as we'd left them. Only the door was missing but Peter had hung a length of carpet in its place, with a hole cut in the top to let in the light, and I liked it better. Carlo came lumbering in and sat down on the settee with a crash and a shout of laughter, making it evident that we were friends again.

'Have you seen my chickens?' he asked. 'I've made a pen for them under the tree. They're still young, of course, but it shouldn't be long before they start laying and then I'll get back what I paid for them. What about that bastard Eric, eh? You know that Blond Helmuth died? Well, Eric took up a collection for a tombstone and what d'you think? The bastard ran off with that as well as my stuff. I'd like to get my hands on him, I can tell you.'

I didn't know Blond Helmuth very well as he'd lived in a squat out of town with Swiss Peter, but it was a surprise to hear that he'd died because he'd always looked so fit. Starved of conversation all summer, Carlo gossiped on and told us, among other trivia, that Uwe had come back to Siracusa and was now in hospital again and Bernd and Wolle didn't sleep in their cave any more because it was so far from the wine house. Eventually Peter climbed into bed for his siesta and only then did Carlo leave.

Life went back to normal and the weather was so good that I usually went into town in the morning as well, partly to avoid Carlo and partly because I wanted to get back into working on the pavement, even if the morning's collection was never as good as in the evening. Then, towards the end of October, the carabinieri (military police) paid us a visit. The Pope was due to spend a day in Siracusa as part of his Sicilian tour in the beginning of November and they warned us that we would have to find alternative accommodation until he left as he was due to give a public address from a point just above our caves and the area was to be cleared for security. They were very helpful.

'You and your wife can go down to the other caves by the Hotel Villa Politi,' they told Peter, 'but Signor Carlo has dogs and chickens so he will have to move out of this area.'

It was very convenient for us, because the big cave was fully furnished so all we had to take were a few clothes and my painting materials. Carlo wasn't so happy, but he found a cave not far from where he'd lived previously and grudgingly moved his menagerie to that over the days that followed.

With the impending visit in mind, I worked hard at doing little portraits of the Pope which we photocopied, mounted and intended to sell cheaply on the street. I also did small pictures in gold and silver on a blue background of the Madonna delle Lacrime and the new church in which she was displayed, the Sanctuary, which was to be given an inaugural blessing by the Pope. Siracusa was thronged with people on the day of the visit and Peter and I gleefully anticipated making far more money than usual, but unfortunately we hadn't considered the presence of other Pope souvenir-sellers and business was sluggish.

We moved back into our caves as soon as the Pope left and a month later Orlando was killed by a car. The big cave was still empty at that time, and one night somebody started a fire inside, destroying all the furniture, books and ornaments that the people had collected over the years and leaving only charred remains and heaps of twisted metal. Peter and I were shocked that anybody could do such a dreadful thing, but Bernd and Wolle were remarkably unmoved by the news and when the weather deteriorated they moved into Lobo's old cave round the corner. Bernd, especially, was vaguer than ever and, although Wolle got butcher's scraps for the dogs when he remembered, it seemed that Goliath was show-

191

ing *them* how to survive on the street, because we frequently saw all three dogs trotting around the town and inspecting the contents of the garbage containers. And then we heard that Uwe had died and I felt supremely guilty for not having taken the trouble to visit him in hospital.

The Santa Lucia festival came and went, profitably for Peter and me, and then it was time for the Father Christmas tour of the town. He wasn't the only one in Siracusa that year, and as we were walking up a street one day, Peter in his costume, we met another Father Christmas coming towards us. They shook hands solemnly and went into a bar, where Peter played 'Jingle Bells' on his kazoo and the other Father Christmas tolled his bell in time to the music. Apart from a small boy who stared in confused awe from one to the other, the other people in the bar were almost splitting their sides with the unrestrained mirth so typical of Italians and, as the Father Christmases shook hands again and went their separate ways, we could still hear the laughter following us down the street.

We had a quiet Christmas, apart from the habitual Christmas morning get-together in Russo's wine house, followed by another in Mario's, but we invited Carlo to a traditional English roast dinner, which I cooked and which was perfect, and spent the rest of the day sleeping and playing cards. New Year's Eve, too, was quieter than usual without the crowd in the big cave, and once again we played cards with Carlo, Peter's one concession to the event being the setting off of three rockets that he'd bought and his gruff 'I loff you, Baby-Prue' as he kissed me to welcome the new year.

Early in January Peter decided to go on one of his solitary whistle-stop tours. As usual I was happy to be on my own with time to read and write instead of working so hard. I didn't really enjoy selling my pictures so I lived frugally, feeding myself and Domino very well on chicken wings (the cheapest meat I could get) and pasta. Admittedly our diet was rather monotonous but Domino was happy enough and I jazzed my own up with a variety of herbs and spices or substituted the meat for beans or lentils. Whatever else, it was healthy as I always had fresh oranges and salad and plenty of milk for my copious mugs of coffee. On my own I very rarely had occasion to go to the wine house, though I bought cheap wine to drink at home and continued to smoke my habitual five or six roll-ups, but I found that I was spending a maximum of 5,000 lire a day, which astounded Carlo.

'Donner wetter!' he exclaimed, his eyes gleaming. 'I need at least 30,000 lire to live! I've got to buy food for myself and all my animals, then there's my newspaper, my lotto, my pools, my cups of coffee out – and I smoke nearly three packets of cigarettes a day. How d'you do it?'

I told him.

'What, chicken wings? No wonder you live cheap, ha, ha, ha. I need proper meat! And I have to have a few coffees in a bar before I start work. And of course it's important to keep doing the lotto and the pools or I'd never have a chance of winning anything. Mmm, I suppose I could cut down on cigarettes. No, no, no, ha, ha, ha, I'd rather work my two hours at the traffic lights every day and live well. I like to enjoy my little luxuries, ha. Ha, ha!'

Occasionally I would run out of cash and would have to go out round the shops with my pictures, but I sold them so cheaply that I had little difficulty in getting rid of most of them. In the end I always enjoyed the excursion because after my first few sales I would begin to feel more confident and, as always, I found everyone so complimentary and charming. Once I had an unusual diversion in a large store selling musical instruments. There was nobody at the counter and, as I looked around me, I heard someone calling out and saw an old man sitting at a piano in the back of the shop. He beckoned me over.

'D'you like music?' I nodded. 'Well, what's this tune then?'

He launched into something that rang a vague bell but I couldn't place it, and when I shook my head he asked me where I came from. I told him, 'England', and he immediately tinkled off 'Land of Hope and Glory' on the keys, humming loudly as he played and calling me to sing along with him. I did so, carolling 'da-de-da' when I couldn't remember the words and the old man was delighted.

'What about this one?' he shouted, plunging into the strains of 'Tipperary', followed by 'Danny Boy', 'Lili Marlene', and 'The Marseillaise' and ordering me to 'sing, sing!' whenever I threatened to falter, 'da-de-daing' along with me in a remarkably powerful tenor voice. I spent a most entertaining hour with him until our musical session was brought to a halt by a customer and I slipped reluctantly away, the old man waving vigorously and exhorting me to come back another day. I intended to.

Three and a half weeks later Peter arrived back, relaxed and cheerful after his spell of freedom. He told me that he'd applied for his passport and had seen Austrian Eric, who'd tried to scrounge a drink off him and been rudely rebuffed; he'd stayed with Thomas in Reggio and heard that Mario had been left a legacy and had bought an old house in Catanzaro; he'd been to Brindisi and had learned that Lapsi was in hospital and Bernd had gone to Taranto, and finally he'd been to Bari to see all his Italian friends.

A few days later Peter was offered work by one of the wine house regulars who had a derelict house in the country and wanted to make it habitable. Peter, Little Natale and Pippo Tedesco were all hired at the going rate of 50,000 lire a day and, even without an alarm clock, Peter had no difficulty in rising at six o'clock in the morning to be down at the meeting point in town. I didn't expect him home till mid-afternoon and was surprised when the three men turned up at our cave before midday, armed with some wine but all looking rather fed up and at a loose end. Peter told me grumpily that when they arrived at the house the electricity had been cut off because the bill hadn't been paid so the machines couldn't run and therefore they couldn't work. Next morning Peter rose with the dawn once more and hastened off to the meeting point, this time returning alone and disconsolate as I was having my breakfast. Oh, dear. The boss just hadn't turned up so another day was lost.

So Peter went out to sell my pictures and was promised faithfully by his wine house that there would be work for him the next day. So off he went as usual in the early morning and, to my amazement, he returned at teatime, wreathed in smiles and in possession of 50,000 lira. We had a relaxed evening in the wine house with an equally happy Pippo and Natale and the following morning Peter rose with the lark yet again. The three friends returned to the cave around mid-morning, and I asked what had happened. This time there had been a police check on all vehicles and as Peter's boss had no papers, he didn't want to risk taking the van out. The following day, however, Peter again returned to the cave while I was having breakfast and this time he was seething. His boss had once more failed to turn up and as far as he was concerned their working relationship was finished.

Spring came and once again all the wild flowers burst into bloom, and the hillside was alive with birdsong and the gentle humming of the bees as they collected their honey. A robin had become friendly and would flirt and twitter on the washing line until I threw him something more interesting than bread. One day, Carlo came home in a great tizzy. He'd met a policeman who'd told him that the area was to be turned into an archaeological zone and we were all to be moved out. Since nobody had said anything to us, we told Carlo not to worry about it, but he was a great respecter of authority and immediately started to search for alternative accommodation. He was lucky enough to be offered the use of a house in the country-side about fifteen kilometres from Siracusa where he could take all his animals, and all he had to do in return was to look after a pair of horses. He was, he admitted to Peter, rather uneasy with horses, but he would have to learn to lose his fear as the opportunity was too good to miss, and over the next few weeks he transferred his animals and his belongings to his new home.

The summer had arrived and it was time for us to go to Greece. Taking the overnight train to Brindisi with Domino settled patiently in his basket, we arrived in Casale to find more people living there than usual, including Volker and Otto. We heard, to our surprise, that Wolfgang had also come back in the company of a fellow Austrian but left suddenly with a large sum of money belonging to the man. I was thoroughly disillusioned: first Eric and then Wolfgang. How could people be so unscrupulous as to steal from their friends? We stayed in the squat for a few days, I spending the time watching television with Helmuth or painting watercolours while Peter and Otto went into town together. As always, I was pleased to see Otto for the first few hours but it wasn't long before I was tired of his noisy exuberance. Even Peter became irritated after being woken twice-running at six in the morning by Otto play-ing his kazoo so, as soon as I had enough pictures in the portfolio to give us an unstressful start in Greece, we packed our belongings and took the ferry to Patras.

Peter stayed only one night in the youth hostel as he wanted to go to Kefalonia in advance of me to make sure of a place to live, always hoping that our boat was still intact. When he didn't telephone to tell me otherwise, I prepared to leave the day after. That night I was awoken by a massive rumbling and shuddering, the biggest earth tremor that I'd experienced and which caused Domino to dive into my sleeping bag for safety. There was a slightly less violent secondary tremor and I wondered briefly if I should go outside into the garden, but I decided against it and went back to sleep. Next morning there was still no telephone call from Peter so I assumed that all was well and took the ferry to Sami.

Peter met me at the bus station in Argostoli and told me that our boat had been moved further away from the town and he wasn't sure if I'd want to live there as it was in worse condition than in former years; but if I wasn't happy with it he'd found a derelict house up on the hill behind the town centre. In fact, I was even more captivated with it than before since the boat had been dumped, still on blocks, in a place surrounded by trees and flowering shrubs – a treat for the eyes. The sea was on the other side of the road, and though there was no beach one only had to clamber down over the rocks to swim, and the place was only about five minutes walk further out of town than the boatyard. It was the next best thing to our cave, and Peter beamed at my happiness.

He'd covered the whole thing with huge fibreglass builder's sacks, which hung over the missing window and could be pushed aside in place of the door, and he'd acquired an old, rickety ladder so that we could climb in and out. It was airier than before, so my working conditions would probably be pleasanter. Domino settled down at once with his bowls of food and water, and we walked back into town for the first non-working evening, being welcomed back as if we belonged in Argostoli. Everything was the same and I loved it: Ari's cafeneion by the bridge; Mitso and Lefteri's where Peter played cards; Stavro's; Demosthenes; and the Pub Old House, and everywhere we kept bumping into people that we knew from before.

Peter rented a motorbike again and our way of life was better than ever. The area round our boat was so pretty that I painted countless views of the landscape in each direction, and if I got too hot I simply crossed the road to swim in the water off the rocks. I loved waking up in the morning before the cicadas, when it was slightly cooler and the sea looked like a mirror. There was a woman, Greek I think, who came down at that hour to sit on the memorial overlooking the water, and she always sang, clearly and melodiously, as she doled out butcher's scraps to the stray dogs who waited for her. Peter got up and went off to a cafeneion for his breakfast when she arrived, but I liked to sit there, sipping my cold coffee and listening to the singing until her husband came to collect her in his car. That was the signal for me to start work, squatting on a footstool and painting at a table that Peter had nailed to the wall for stability. The boat was never as comfortable as the cave inside, but otherwise it was even more idyllic, with the sea so close by as well as the beauty of nature and the oregano, dill and wild thyme growing all around so that I had fresh herbs to cook with. I loved the ceaseless 'chack-chacking' of the cicadas as I worked, and the aromatic walk into town through the pine trees and eucalyptus gave me so much pleasure that, more often than before, I came into town around midday to meet Peter for a few beers at lunchtime.

We spent a lot more time together than before because Peter wanted my company when he went into Lassi in the evenings. Instead of always going to the music bars, he found that he did his best business in the restaurants, and I was quite content to sit sipping a glass of wine while he did his selling. I think it was his rich guttural accent and convoluted way with words that sold my pictures more than anything else. If people were interested, Peter would enlarge on the theme, sometimes telling little stories (often invented) about the pictures and talking about Domino and our boat. The mention of the boat frequently led people to assume that we lived on a yacht in the harbour and it was always with a certain amount of amusement that Peter explained that this was not the case.

As a sideline to selling pictures, Peter took to giving regular fire-shows in some of the bars. He welcomed any change from selling and when Makis and Lefteris of the Pub Old House asked him to paint some murals on their cruise boat, he did so with gusto. Although I probably worked a lot harder in the summer, Kefalonia was a holiday time for me, partly because I got the chance to regularly speak English and partly because we made enough money for luxuries, such as buying newspapers and eating out whenever we wanted.

But by October, Peter was beginning to yearn to be amongst Italian-speaking people once more and we decided to go home. Unsure as to whether we'd be able to occupy our cave again, he left first so that he could find alternative accommodation if necessary, and I followed with the ever-patient Domino so that I could stop overnight in both Patras and Casale to allow him a little freedom.

17 Introduction to Crete

The ferry journey to Brindisi wasn't as comfortable as usual since it was a smaller ship and there were no Pullman seats, and I had to sleep outside on the metal deck with Domino. Then there was a secondary hiccup in the transfer from the docking quay to the main port. There was a tiny ferry that transported foot passengers across and, being rather overloaded with my cumbersome ruck-sack, I tripped as I was going down the steps and the little nylon sack containing my sleeping-bag and jacket flew out of my hand and vanished into the murky water. As I lurched to grab at the handrail with one hand, clutching tightly to Domino's basket with the other, I overbalanced completely and landed on my back with my top half on the boat, my legs on the quay and my bottom hanging over the water. Still holding Domino aloft, I was heaved into the boat by able-bodied passengers, while the ferryman delved into the sea with his boat-hook and brought up the dripping and stinking nylon sack. All was well at the other end as I was helped out and my luggage passed to me item by item, and I made my way to Casale without further mishap.

Helmuth greeted me comfortably and invited me to help myself to wine and there was a good film that we could watch on the television. During the commercial breaks he told me that Lapsi had died in hospital and it was suspected that Bernd had died also since Caspar, the dog, who'd always been his companion, had been seen with someone else in Taranto. Lapsi had always looked frail, but Bernd had been the opposite and I wondered if someone could

199

have stolen Caspar. Helmuth thought it unlikely. He was still taking valium, I noticed.

'Well, it helps me to sleep,' he said. 'I get it on prescription. The only trouble is that I have to hide it from Stefan, because he's capable of gulping the lot in one go.'

I could believe that, as Stefan was definitely not normal. I went into Brindisi next morning to buy some chicken and vegetables for a stew, and when I came back I found that there were four smart plastic chairs in the kitchen instead of the wooden bench and the old stools. When Ossie came in he stared at them suspiciously and asked me where they came from, and, of course, I'd no idea so he called Stefan and demanded to know if he knew anything about them.

'I found them last night,' said the lad innocently.

'They're from the pizzeria opposite, aren't they, hah?' Oscar looked as grim as his amiable face would allow.

'Well, yes, but where's the problem, Ossie? After all, they've got plenty of others.'

'I'll tell you what the problem is. We have to live here and we don't want the locals regarding us as thieves. You'll have to take them back, hah.'

'Oh, Ossie, but they look so nice,' pleaded Stefan. 'Can't we keep them?'

Oscar was adamant and stood there severely until Stefan stacked the chairs and accompanied him, grumbling, to the pizzeria. I stayed in the squat for one more night and then I considered that Peter had had enough time to sort out our cave or whatever, and took the train to Siracusa.

Peter met me at Russo's, and we walked up to the cave together, he shouldering my rucksack and telling me the latest gossip and I carrying the ever-patient Domino. One bit of news that really shook me, since I'd known them for so long, was that Bernd and Wolle had both died during the summer, Wolle on the way to hospital and Bernd found as stiff as a board in the park one morning. I found it horrifying how many of our friends had died!

I had little time to relax as in my absence Peter had got me several orders for pictures of Santa Lucia and it was nice to have money coming in so quickly. Then, at the beginning of December, as I was sitting in the cave and painting, I got paid a visit by a contingent of civil servants from the Town Hall. They gazed around, admired my picture and informed me that regrettably, our cave was needed for a Nativity play that was to be enacted over the Christmas period, when the whole of the hillside was going to be turned into Bethlehem. We would have to find other accommodation for a few weeks and take our furniture with us because 'they didn't have gas cookers in Biblical times, ha, ha'.

When I told Peter he was unperturbed except for the thought of having to move all the furniture which had been difficult enough to install in the first place, what with the rocks and ditches all round us. We looked at Lobo's old cave but that was in too horrible a state to consider staying for more than a night or two so we stayed where we were and hoped that something would turn up. Eventually an exasperated council official allowed us to store our furniture in the back room that Carlo had built into his cave and Signor Buonanno, one of the wine house regulars, offered Peter a room in his house. It was only about a hundred metres from Natale so we moved down there with a rucksack full of essentials and Domino in his basket. I have to say that although it was kind of Buonanno to let us stay with him, I hated living in his house. Privacy was nil since when he was drunk, which was most days, he would think nothing of barging into our room, unannounced, to talk to Peter, and apart from that, his house was dirty and stank of cats. Domino didn't mind because Buonanno's cat was a female and there were more females in the street outside to tickle his fancy, and Peter could tolerate it because there was a television in the house so he got the chance to watch a film every night. We stayed there for the duration of the Santa Lucia festival and I spent as little time as possible in the house, working outside the church throughout the day; but as the Christmas holiday approached I dreaded the thought of not being able to work and of being confined to the house unless I spent all day in the wine house with Peter. Peter understood how I felt and urged me to go to England to stay with my mother until we could move back into our cave, and I loved him for not minding that I'd be away for Christmas.

I came back to Siracusa in January, although Peter had warned me that Domino had disappeared and things were not as nice as before. The latter was an understatement and I was almost in tears to see that not only had a wide pathway been cleared through the rocks all the way up to the caves, but a great chunk of undergrowth had been cut away from the cactus ring, leaving a clear view all the way through to our courtyard and the entrance to our cave. Our little paradise had been ruined. Peter suggested that we stay for a few more weeks in case Domino turned up, but if we couldn't find him it might be a good time to try our luck in Crete, particularly as Otto was reputed to be there now. In February Domino was still absent and we decided not to wait any longer.

All of a sudden I felt the thrill of preparing to be on the move again, of going somewhere new, and the desecration of our home fell into the background of my mind. We packed our rucksacks and took the train to Brindisi, stopping off only at Reggio to spend a night with Thomas and to listen to any street gossip he might have heard. Mario wasn't there and we toyed with the idea of going to Catanzaro, but Thomas wasn't sure whether he'd be there either and, as we didn't want to waste too much time and money, we decided to leave it till we came back to Italy. As Peter said, 'We have time.'

We stayed in Brindisi for a few days but the squat had gone to rack and ruin, with rats and mice everywhere. Helmuth was in a bad way, drinking heavily and dosing himself with valium, going out to beg on Sundays but relying on Oscar to do his shopping for him and spending more time in bed than ever before. Ossie was his usual equable self, going out and about on his bicycle and always smiling, but in addition to the weird Stefan there was only a dissipated-looking Austrian called Hans living in the squat with them. We went to Lecce most days to make money, Peter collecting for me with usual zest as I worked on the pavement, as keen to leave Brindisi as I was. I could put up with many discomforts, but the thing that I found really difficult to accept was the infestation of vermin, and I found it hard to sleep with rats scurrying across the bed throughout the night.

We stayed only briefly in Patras to make the essential social rounds, and then we went to Piraeus to catch the ferry to Crete. We arrived in Souda before daybreak on a bleak, rainy February morning, sitting in a cafeneion for over an hour until the buses to Hania started running. Otto's friend, Michael, ran a Christian group on the island and lived in a village just outside Hania; we had his telephone number and contacted his wife, who told us that Michael and Otto were both in town and we would be able to find them around midday in a little cafeneion by the market. We had time to spare and wandered around, pausing for a drink in several different cafeneions until the rain stopped, and eventually going to our rendezvous point, where we came upon an astonished Otto. He introduced us to his friend and, amid great rejoicing, we explained that funds were strictly limited and we needed to find a cheap place to stay or, preferably, somewhere free. Michael was a quiet, gentle-mannered man, obviously deeply religious and more concerned with the spiritual than the practical side of life, but Otto took the hint.

'Well, I live alone in a little village outside Hania and you could stay with me if you like, but you have to remember that it's a Church house and so there's strictly no smoking and no alcohol.'

'How do you manage, then?' asked Peter artlessly.

'Ah, well, I never smoked much and, of course, I've given up drinking alcohol,' said Otto virtuously, indicating his Fanta. 'It did me no good and I feel so much healthier since I stopped. I'm very involved with the church now, aren't I, Michael?'

'Yes, indeed, he's a great help to me,' Michael agreed. 'Otto more or less runs the Bible study evening. You must come to it, Peter, I think you'd enjoy it and there's always a free meal afterwards and you can have a shower if you want to. We have a lot of young people coming. It was all Otto's idea.'

We chatted for a while longer until Michael got up to go, after which Otto relaxed visibly and became quite expansive as he boasted about all that he did for Michael's church, and how so many more people were coming to it since he started organizing things. He had two jobs walking dogs for members of Michael's congregation, and he was never short of money.

He took us round the old part of Hania on the sea side of the market, pointing out the places that might interest us: a German bar, a second-hand shop and so on. It was an attractive old town, full of narrow, winding little streets reminiscent of Italy and with a picturesque harbour surrounded by countless dormant restaurants. As we passed a crumbling building on which work was in progress, we were hailed from above and Rene, from Catania, came hurrying down to greet us. He was married now, he told us, but his wife had gone back to Yugoslavia for a few weeks and we were welcome to stay with him until we got ourselves sorted out. So we did, but he had a large and over-friendly dog and I found it impossible to do my painting, so as soon as we'd found a cheap pension we moved in there. Despite the fact that Crete was so far south, we were surprised to find that it was bitterly cold and I was thankful for the thick woollen underwear that we'd been given in Brindisi, something that we'd never needed in Siracusa. It rained continuously, as well, so there was no opportunity to search for a squat. Business, however, was generally very good and, even though his customers were all locals, Peter managed to sell enough of my paintings every day for us to live surprisingly well.

We liked the Cretans. There was something proud but unsophisticated about them, very genuine and kind, and I liked the traditional costume that the older men from the villages often wore, although I never understood the significance of jodhpurs and riding boots when they didn't appear to ride horses. I also liked the fact that, unlike in most parts of Greece, the stray cats and dogs of Hania looked as well-fed as they did in Italy. We used to frequent a tiny cafeneion run by a lively young couple called Yiannis and Nectaria. It was the cheapest place in town and there was almost always a baked potato to go with ouzo or wine, so on the days when business was bad it was still possible to have enough to eat at the same time as imbibing, and the atmosphere was invariably cheery and full or argument and laughter. There were other good cafeneions too, as well as Otto's German bar (so called because Ina, the young girl who ran it was German), and these were all part of Peter's daily walkabout in Splantzia, the less fashionable part of the old town. When it came to selling we went to the more trendy and up-market area around the harbour, also nice in its own way and very tastefully done up, but very much more expensive.

Towards the end of March the weather cleared and Peter resumed his search for somewhere for us to live for free, eventually finding a little hut on the beach at Ayia Marina, about ten kilometres out of town. It was perfect for us and we got the permission of the owner to live there and moved in straight away. There was a table and some shelves inside, and over the days that followed Peter acquired some old chairs and made a bed out of planks raised off the floor on bricks. There was a cafeneion in the village, which was ten minutes walk inland through shady olive groves and up a hill and, as the tourist season began to get under way, the whole of the area along the coast started to burst into life as all the bars, tavernas and restaurants opened up for the summer. Peter needed a motorbike more than ever and was lucky enough to be offered one, second-hand, by a cafeneion acquaintance, and from then on it was no problem to go into the village first and then cover the long stretch of tourist attractions on the main road. Most of the tourists in the area were Scandinavian, and business was reasonably good, but Peter missed the cafeneion life of Hania, which was too far to visit after work, and there was hardly anywhere that I really enjoyed spending the evening, the whole area being geared towards tourism. After weighing up the pros and cons, we decided to wait till June and then go back to Kefalonia where there was more of a mix between the local and the tourist life.

One evening in the middle of May, we got a message from

Michael to say that my mother had died and the following day I sadly flew back to England for the funeral, glad only that chance had enabled me to be with her at Christmas.

I had arranged to meet Peter in Kefalonia, though I didn't get there till the middle of June, relieved to see him and to feel his comforting arms round me as he told me how much he loved me. Our boat was where it had been the previous year – a little more decayed, certainly, but still intact. He'd sold the rest of my pictures and given several fire-shows to augment his income, but he was happy that I was back before he'd got too deeply in debt. I told him that in due course I would have some income from my mother's 'estate', which would take the pressure off us financially, but Peter said gruffly that he wasn't interested in my money and we would earn our living as we always had done. And we did.

Life went back to normal as I painted during the day and went out selling with Peter at night. We went swimming together, we went for trips on the motorbike, we loved, we laughed and all the time I felt so lucky to be with him, enjoying to the full each moment as it came. But as the summer gradually went by and July slipped into August, I started to notice things that worried me. Peter seemed to be eating far less than was normal for him and yet he was drinking more and sleeping much later, and I often heard him retching in the morning, something he'd never done before. Then his desire to sell pictures diminished and what had been fun became a chore, and towards the end of August he told me that he wanted to leave as the time had come for him to do something about his alcohol problem.

He'd talked about it before and I was glad that he'd finally made his decision, which seemed to have taken a weight off his mind and he was as happy as I'd ever seen him. We went straight back to Patras and Peter outlined his plans, telling me that he would sell his motorbike first and then we would 'make the street' to Konstanz, in Germany, where he would check into the clinic and I would go back to England until he was 'clean'. The process might take up to six months, but that was nothing compared to a lifetime, and afterwards we'd have an even better time together than before, and what did I think? Naturally I agreed with him.

206

While we were waiting to sell the motorbike Otto arrived unexpectedly at the youth hostel, telling us defiantly that he was finished with Crete. His position as organizer of the Bible study evenings had been usurped by another German so now he could go back to his vagabond life, which was more to his taste. Having shed his pious veneer he wanted Peter to go out merrymaking with him, and every evening they did the rounds of the bars and cafeneions busking with their kazoos. At last someone came up with the money for Peter's motorbike and, with a comforting surplus of money in our pockets, we were able to leave for Italy.

We didn't stay long in Casale even though the squat had been freed of rats, because Helmuth was barely aware of us and Peter wanted to be on his way to Germany as soon as possible. We spent one day in Lecce and another in Bari to see his friends, and then Peter was ready to leave, taking the same route as when we'd been deported. We arrived in Konstanz five days later. It took some time to make the necessary arrangements for Peter and meanwhile we slept comfortably in an empty goods-wagon at the station and spent the evenings going round the bars to sell my remaining watercolours. It seemed only a few days later that Peter was told to check in at the clinic and I reluctantly took the train for England.

18   Peter's Wine House

I came back to Konstanz in late November. Peter had telephoned me to say that he was in hospital, and then telephoned again to say that he'd checked himself out and he'd explain later. He met me at the station, enveloping me in his arms, burying his face in my hair and kissing me hungrily. He took me for a beer and his news wasn't good. He had lung cancer, he said, and the doctors weren't certain that surgery would be successful. As things were he had two years to live and so he'd decided to spend one more year on the road with me, and afterwards he'd let the doctors do whatever they wanted.

I was stunned but I understood his feelings, understood how, after so many years of freedom on the road, he dreaded the thought of being restricted in any way, and whatever he wanted to do I would go along with him and help him in any way I could. He said that the first thing was to go back to Sicily. We'd stay in Siracusa for the Santa Lucia festival, maybe spend Christmas in Reggio and New Year in Brindisi, and afterwards we'd see. Maybe we'd try Crete again. I wanted nothing more than to be with him.

We slept that night in the railway wagon and the next day we took the train to Reggio Calabria. Of all the friends we knew well it seemed that only Thomas remained and now he was living with a young Swiss girl, Claudia. It was clear that he was pleased to see us and, in his usual gruff manner, he invited us to stay for as long as we liked. We only stayed for a few days but it was fun. Peter wanted to see all his Italian friends, so we visited the different bars and wine houses in Reggio, sometimes on our own and sometimes with Thomas and Claudia, who was a sweet girl with a gentle personality. Most evenings we played cards and Thomas taught us how to play canasta, a game which we took up with enthusiasm. Thomas was as serious about card games as Carlo had been and it was important to him to win, although Peter and I seemed to have an unfair share of luck, because we usually won. Claudia, it must be said, wasn't as quick on the uptake as she might have been and we'd often be witnesses to the most toe-curling exchanges, Thomas having a naturally ferocious manner:

'Now then, Claudia, if you've got a run put it down, d'you understand?'

'Yes, Thomas, but I haven't got a run yet.'

'Are you sure? Check your cards again. You must have one by now.'

'But Thomas, really I haven't.'

'Now, you're not trying, Claudia. You've got to concentrate.'

So it would go on, and a little while later Claudia would put down several runs all at the same time and Thomas would go almost berserk, while Peter and I would be avoiding each other's eyes for fear of laughing outright.

In the first week of December, after promising them that we'd see them some time over the Christmas period, we decided to go back to Siracusa in good time for the Santa Lucia festival, as we had no idea if our cave would still be free and it was essential to find somewhere to stay before the onset of the cold weather. As soon as we got off the train we walked along to Russo's to leave our rucksacks, have a drink and hear the latest gossip. His mouth dropped open when he saw us.

'Peter, you're alive! It's a miracle! We heard that you were dead!'

'No,' said Peter dryly, 'not yet. Who told you that?'

From the description, 'the Austrian with the limp', we gathered that it must have been Wolfgang and asked Russo to tell him that we'd see him later. Mario and Natale had closed for lunch and so we made our way up to the caves. To our dismay, our own little cave had been completely wrecked inside and was full of old litter, and there was a group of Yugoslavians in the one next door. They were pleasant enough and we chatted with them for a few minutes before going down the hill to see if what had been Lobo's cave was habitable, only to find that it was in as bad a state as ours. The weather was still warm so we decided to sleep in the open on a rock ledge outside the big cave where we'd lived originally and next day we'd look for somewhere better to stay. When it was time for the wine houses to open we wandered back down to Natale.

'Lazarus!'

That was Peter's first greeting, but everyone was overjoyed that he was still alive and apparently well. When we got to Mario's there was the same astounded reaction and it appeared that Wolfgang had made a collection for a tombstone. Padre Rufino was as amazed as everyone else and embraced Peter with happiness.

'You've put me in a very embarrassing position, you realize,' he chided Peter affectionately. 'I said a Mass for you last week and now I'm going to have to announce that it was all a mistake.'

When we got back to Russo's to collect our rucksacks we weren't surprised to find that Wolfgang had already left Siracusa. We slept in the open for three nights, unable to find anywhere better, and then Mario offered us the use of his old flat, which was still partially furnished although there was no electricity. We moved in gratefully and although it was dark and cold in comparison to our cave, it was clean, comfortable and conveniently in the centre of town, and much more agreeable than Buonanno's house. Padre Ruffino gave us candles and we soon got back into our old way of life. Peter got me orders for pictures that I could paint at home, sitting at the table in the kitchen, and when the Santa Lucia festival started I spent most of the day at the church, doing my pictures on the ground while Peter collected for me more animatedly than he'd done for years. We decided to celebrate New Year in Brindisi and left Siracusa on Christmas Day after the standard get-together in the sunshine outside Russo's wine house, something that both Peter and I thought of as an essential part of the Christmas festivities. It was almost like a renewing of friendships and the only difference was that for the first time we were the only foreigners there, the last of the cavemen. It felt quite strange.

We went to Reggio to stay with Thomas and Claudia and had

211

such a sociable time that we were easily persuaded to stay for New Year's Eve, drinking sparkling wine outside the squat as we watched the fireworks exploding all over Reggio and in Messina, on the other side of the straits. Peter kissed me and his blue eyes gazed into mine, intent and happy. This was the end of our seventh year together, he said, the 'accursed' seventh year, and from now on life would get better. I loved him more than ever at that point and prayed that he was right. Although our love for each other was as deep as ever, what with Domino's disappearance, the ruining of our cave, the death of my mother and finally the dreadful news of Peter's cancer, 1996 had not been the best year of our lives. I prayed fervently that 1997 would be luckier for us, that God might perform a miracle and restore Peter's good health so that he could continue his vagabond life with me for many years to come.

The following evening we took the train to Brindisi and arrived in Casale to find the squat in a state of chaos, with broken glass all over the kitchen floor. Ossie was there sweeping it up and he told us grimly that their New Year's Eve party had culminated in Otto and Hans deciding that it would be a lark to follow the Greek custom of breaking plates, fortunately substituting the plates with beer bottles. The unimaginative Hans was easily manipulated by the gregarious and mischievous Otto and naturally neither of them had thought to clean up the mess afterwards. We were sorry to hear that Helmuth had died, but not really surprised as he'd been in such a bad way on our last visit. We were interrupted by raucous shouts and the tooting of a kazoo as Otto and Hans, already inebriated, came tramping in with a crate of beer, which they set down with a crash.

'Peter!' shouted Otto boisterously. 'You're back! When are we going to do the aeroplane number?'

Peter grinned at the memory of their plans to beg on an aeroplane and the two men launched into their usual animated repartee, punctuated at intervals by Otto's tuneless blasts on his kazoo and Hans's inane cackles of laughter. Ossie disappeared and Volker put his head round the door to greet us but didn't stay. By the time Otto had finished three beers and retired for an early siesta I was already weary of his company, and I was further disenchanted by

212

the spectacle of Hans excavating his nostrils, the contents of which he studied with absorbed curiosity. We went out for a pizza and Peter admitted that with Hans as a willing disciple, Otto seemed even more extrovert and loud than before, an opinion reinforced over the next two days when we were routinely awoken before daybreak by Otto's barging into our room and blowing raspberries on the kazoo. Old friend though he may have been, I deeply resented this uncouth invasion of our privacy, apart from which the lack of sleep left me tired and irritable. I complained bitterly to Peter who, by this time was as fed up as I was with these constant disruptions, and we packed our rucksacks and took the ferry to Greece.

When we arrived in Crete at the beginning of January, Peter had little idea of what he wanted to do beyond hoping that Michael might be able to help him by letting us stay in a church house, and perhaps introducing him to people so that he could take over some of the jobs that Otto had done. Both Michael and his wife were disconcerted by Peter's news but explained regretfully that the houses had already been reoccupied and Otto's work had long since been reallocated, although they would, of course, bear Peter in mind if anything came up. Not too disappointed, we took a bus out to Ayia Marina and were piqued to discover that our little hut on the beach had been reclaimed by the owner and converted back into an office.

So we went back to the modest pension we'd lived in when we first came to Crete, and I did my painting on the bedside cabinet, on which I also cooked up cheap meals on our camping-gas burner. We continued to drink in the tiny cafeneion by the market and subsisted on Nectaria's baked potatoes when business was bad. One day my brother telephoned me to give me the welcome news that our mother's house had been sold and my share of the proceeds had been paid into the bank, and the same evening we learned that Ina, who had the 'German' bar, wanted to get out of the licensing trade. Being wintertime our own business hadn't been going too well, and I tentatively suggested to Peter that if we took over the bar I could continue to do my painting, we could sleep in the room upstairs and we would thus have two sources of income.

213

Knowing his love for the free life, I never thought he'd give my proposition even the slightest consideration but to my surprise he jumped at the idea. He'd always wanted to run a bar, he said, and it would mean that when he eventually went back to Germany and put himself in the hands of the 'medicine men', I would have a source of income.

So we did the deal with Ina and moved out of the pension and into the bar, sleeping (on flattened cardboard boxes, naturally) on the floor of the room above. We decided to put the licence in Peter's name since there was a German consulate in Hania, enabling the transaction to go through without any hitches and, on my instigation, we called it Peter's Wine House. Our plan was to run a cafeneion instead of a bar, a cheap and friendly little place  where both Greeks and tourists would feel at home, and Peter was in his element, painting colourful murals on the walls to give it character and thinking up ideas to please the customers, such as giving a sweet biscuit with tea or coffee. A free meze (small plate of food, like tapas) with ouzo or wine was obligatory, of course. The one unforeseen aggravation was that it was more tiring than either of us had anticipated, mostly due to the unexpectedly long opening hours. Due to the fact that in Ina's day it had been open only in the evenings, the people who knew it were used to coming in late at night and staying until three or four in the morning, which was not in our plan at all since we were open from eight o'clock in the morning and had hoped to close no later than midnight. Unfortunately, until people accepted this, we had no choice but to work through until all the customers had left as we needed the money, and it took ages for people to realize that we were open all day. As a result, although we closed for a desperately needed siesta

214

in the afternoon, we were always very short of sleep in those first few months.

We had a large and thoroughly international clientele, including a lot of Greeks, some Arabs and a miscellany of nationalities from all over Western and Eastern Europe, nice people in the majority. Then we had our first problem, only a week after we'd opened, when a malignant little German-speaking Greek by the name of Yiannis got very drunk and tried to smash up the bar. He didn't like Peter, he screamed, and would ensure that the cafeneion was closed within a week. I was very upset by the incident but Peter calmed me down and assured me that the man didn't have everything in the head and we'd have no further trouble with him. We didn't and our cafeneion remained open.

After that incident things went well on the whole. I experimented with different recipes to make cheap and tasty snacks to go with the ouzo and wine, producing little dishes of spicy liver, fried fish, curry or potato salad and never realizing that cooking on the premises was illegal under a cafeneion licence as was sleeping in the room upstairs. Nobody told us, everybody enjoyed the food and nobody tried to stop up, even though we were working completely without a licence for seven months. We seemed to be under some sort of protective umbrella since, although we were visited by the police from time to time, we were never harassed and we were never put in the cells, an event that we were assured was inevitable for a foreigner trying to run a bar. The police were always courteous with us and seemed perfectly willing to accept our excuse that the reason we didn't have our licence was that the town hall was being dilatory in processing our papers. This happened to be true, and Peter or I visited the appropriate departments on a twice-weekly basis to try to galvanize them, unsuccessfully, into action. We'd been told by various German and English friends that sooner or later we would be bound to fall foul of the law, but the worst we experienced was a small fine for making too much noise.

I can only think that we were allowed to carry on untroubled by authority because Peter had such a wonderful relationship with the Greeks in the area. He loved them, preferring their company even to that of his own people and spending almost more time in the cafeneions of his Greek friends than he did in his own. I complained to him once, quivering with indignation after a particularly busy period on my own, that we should have called it 'Prue's Cafeneion' since I was the one who was in it most of the time, and after that he made sure that he was there whenever the place got crowded. The mornings were usually quiet and I was happy to be on my own even though I never found the time to do my painting, but in the evenings I liked having back-up, if only to deal with difficult customers.

Unfortunately, because we were foreigners ourselves and our bar prices were cheap, we attracted a lot of foreign riff-raff. In fact they were a minority, but due to the unpleasantness they caused by upsetting our normal customers with their drunkenness and aggression, they seemed a major problem. Many of these people were charming when sober, but nevertheless they had to be barred and, slowly but surely, the cafeneion took on the relaxed and cheery atmosphere that both men and women enjoyed. We had our difficulties, too, one of which arose from various individuals trying to borrow money and running up bar bills, because getting paid back was a never-ending struggle, nobody seeming to appreciate or care that we had our own bills to pay. Most of the foreigners had financial or other problems, but neither Peter nor I had ever come across quite so many who seemed unable to cope without drinking heavily and becoming aggressive, tearful or simply lunatic. We'd lived for so long in the company of alcoholics and vagabonds and yet the behaviour of those people, who had so little in life, was a lot more normal than that of many of our customers. The good thing was that the problem people didn't all come in at the same time.

To Peter's great pleasure, Otto came back to Crete, though he was only on a short visit this time as he'd managed to find work in Germany. Work? Neither Peter nor I could take this seriously. Was this the same Otto who'd always proudly boasted that he'd never done a day's work in his life? He put our minds at rest by explaining smugly that he'd passed his driving test at last and, as his job was as a driver, it wasn't like work at all, no more so than running a cafeneion. ('Hah!' I thought cynically.) It was like the old days, listening to the two of them arguing and laughing as they played their kazoos and recalled times past, even rehashing their plans for begging on an aeroplane. But the time soon came for Otto to go back to Germany and, for once in our lives, both Peter and I were quite sorry to see him go.

After he left we were busy until the end of April, and then things quietened a lot as the tourist season got under way. We still had our regulars but a lot of the East Europeans, who were among our best customers, found evening work in the many tavernas and restaurants that had opened up for the summer, and our takings reflected this gap. We had hoped to attract tourists as there were so many passing down our street, but very few stopped as it was stiflingly hot in the town and they nearly all wanted to sit down by the harbour. To drum up trade, Peter decided to give a fire-show, making it a regular thing if necessary. I tried to dissuade him as it seemed a crazy thing to do in view of his malady, but he refused to listen to me, saying that he wasn't a cripple yet. That was Peter.

I couldn't argue him out of it so I made him a new costume out of an old black tracksuit and he gave his fire-show in the bar to the music of 'Bolero', the strains of which echoed down the street as he performed. The customers loved it and he gave another show a week later, inadvertently setting fire to the wooden framework of the door and having to beat it out to howls of delight from the customers. I was glad when, after a few weeks, normal business started to pick up again and Peter discontinued his fire-shows, as I took no pleasure out of seeing him abuse his body more than necessary.

Peter never complained of pain, or anything else for that matter, and I think that the general stress of running the cafeneion took his mind, to a large degree, off the unpleasant fact that he had cancer. But as the months went by he began to experience difficulty in sleeping, his breathing becoming increasingly laboured unless he was in an upright position. At last he realized that the time had come to go back to Germany and, until he returned, I was to keep the cafeneion going on my own. He refused to fly, insisting on taking the land route via Patras and Brindisi even though it would take longer, because he might never be able to 'make the street' again, and it was important to him because he was a vagabond at heart.

He refused to let me go down to the bus stop with him as he hated long drawn out partings and firmly kissed me goodbye at the door of the cafeneion before shouldering his rucksack and striding off down the road.

I kept the cafeneion open exactly as Peter wanted, helped when necessary by two of my English friends, and I was so busy that I had no time to brood over Peter's absence. He called me as soon as he was admitted to hospital so that I could keep in touch and I telephoned him regularly. One evening, a month after he'd left and without any warning, he suddenly returned! The change in him in the short time he'd been away was frightening and he was almost unrecognizable as the optimistic character that I'd waved goodbye to as he'd marched off to the bus stop. The cancer must have spread to his larynx because he could speak in little more than a whisper, and his eyes had a desperate, hopeless expression in them that tore at my heart.

We went to his doctor next morning and, after reading through the papers that he'd been given, she confirmed my innermost fear that there had been no operation and told me that nothing could be done except for Peter to take drugs to alleviate any pain. Determined to try everything Peter insisted on seeing the lung specialist, a Greek woman who told him that there was no way of halting the cancer but that he should go into hospital where at least he could be looked after properly. He refused.

But from then on he refused to eat, as if to hasten the inevitable, and though he took the morphine as prescribed, he spent more time than ever in the cafeneions where his Greek friends drank. I wanted to be with him all the time, but he insisted that I continue to run his cafeneion as usual and even tried to help me, though the drugs altered his conception of time and he would often close up early in the evening and then try to reopen again in the middle of the night. I existed on catnaps, never knowing when Peter might do something strange, and all the time I forced myself to behave as if everything was all right so that he wouldn't worry about me. One day he bought me a ring, putting it on my finger and murmuring 'I have want go married with you, Baby,' and often he would sit across the table from me, reach for my hand and whisper, with the hint of his old smile, 'Baby-Prue, I loff you.' I would be in anguish as I kissed him and smiled back, 'Not as much as I love you.' All our friends rallied round to help me but I have to say that without the support of the Greeks and their kindness to Peter I don't think I could have carried on.

My daughter arrived a week later and took a lot of the pressure off me, taking it in turns with me to go out with him or stay behind the bar in the cafeneion. Peter had always loved Kate as if she were his own daughter, and he welcomed her happy-go-lucky presence as much as I did. Warning me how important my welfare was to him and how he would hate to see me unhappy, she made me see humour in the bleakest situations so that I'd laugh instead of crying, and with her to help me it was easier to keep cheerful. All the same, I felt as if I were in the deepest hell as I watched him deteriorate slowly, day after day getting a little worse, his mind wandering at times so that he wasn't even sure where he was. I was walking hand-in-hand with him, coming back from another cafeneion and Peter whispered to me that we must get back to the boat as we couldn't leave Domino on his own. My heart felt like breaking as I replied gently, 'Yes, darling, we'll go home tomorrow.'

He survived for forty days after coming back to Hania, even though after a while he refused to take all medication. His mind cleared a bit so that he knew what was happening, and yet he never once complained of pain or showed any self-pity. He continued with his habitual round of the cafeneions, always ending up in his own, and I prayed that he would die sitting there with a wine on the table, his friends around him and his German music playing in the background. But he had no such luck and continued to hang on day after day until eventually he became so weak that, even with my help, he was unable to get off the mattress on the floor upstairs and lay there gazing through the window, his eyes still as blue as the sky outside. He had to leave me, he whispered, it was a 'bullshit' but there was nothing he could do.

It was never more difficult to keep the tears from overflowing as I lay beside him, holding him in my arms and kissing him, telling him how much I loved him and all the time wishing that I could die myself. I was awoken the following morning by Peter thrashing from side to side in some sort of fit, and there wasn't anything that his doctor could do for him except to telephone for an ambulance to take him to the hospital. I can only hope that he was aware of nothing at that stage. The ambulance men came upstairs and carried him down to the stretcher as if he were a sack of potatoes, one heaving him up by the shoulders and the other taking his legs. At Hania hospital he was rushed to an emergency ward where screaming harridans in white coats plugged him into a machine and hurled questions at me: 'Why is he like this? Why is he so thin? Why? Why? Why?' I answered as best I could, watching the man I loved lying there attached to the electrodes, his life ebbing away. 'Peter, my darling, I love you,' I cried and one of the harridans screeched at me, 'You stupid woman, he can't hear you. Can't you see he's in a coma?' And then Peter died, everything stopped and the ghoul in the white coat picked up one of Peter's legs and dropped it a couple of times, just to make sure. 'He's dead, can't you see,' she snapped when I asked if I might kiss him, but I was allowed that favour and closed his eyes for him myself, overcome with a feeling of intense loss combined with relief that at last his suffering was over and he was at peace.

Burials take place quickly in Greece so I had no time to mourn, but ran from one place to another to get the death certificate from Peter's doctor, inform the sprightly undertaker and make the arrangements for the funeral. I was refused a burial plot by the Greek Orthodox Church, but the priest at the Catholic Church went out of his way to give me whatever help and comfort I needed. The funeral was arranged for the following morning and I was allotted a prepared grave and given a key to the cemetery.

Stavros, who owned a cafeneion on the opposite side of the road and had always been there when we needed help, came across that evening to pay his respects and to find out when the funeral was to take place. I told him.

'Where is Peter at the moment?' he asked.

'He's up at the hospital. The hearse is taking him from there to the cemetery.'

220

'Right, you and your daughter be ready at half past nine tomorrow morning and we'll go up to the hospital together.'

'But Stavro, I promised to be at the cemetery at ten o'clock to open the gates.'

'Look, I know what I'm doing and *you will come to the hospital with me*. Have you got that?'

Who was I to argue? Stavros obviously did know more about such situations than I did, so Kate and I duly presented ourselves at the appointed time and sat chatting to his uncle, a kind old man who kept sighing and regretting Peter's death, telling us that he had often been warned of the dangers of drinking ouzo without eating a meze at the same time. At a quarter to ten Stavros appeared, and to this day I remain infinitely grateful for his presence. He drove us to the hospital, at breakneck speed through all the narrow little side streets of Hania, knowing exactly where to go, fortunately, and taking me straight to the 'dead room', an open room which backed onto where all the hospital traffic turned, belching out diesel fumes, and in which there were several wooden tables and one corpse.

'Is that Peter?' asked Stavros, and I checked, nodding 'Yes.'

'Well, where's the undertaker then?' he barked. 'The funeral's supposed to be at half past ten.'

I gave him the telephone number and we could hear him shouting down the line and demanding to know why Peter wasn't already in his coffin.

'No problem, we'll be there in ten minutes,' was the unflustered reply, so the four of us stood at the hospital entrance, drinking coffee, smoking and waiting for our hearse. It started to rain heavily. A hearse drove in and we moved forward eagerly, but it wasn't ours, and in due course it drove out again. Our hearse arrived seven minutes before the funeral service was due to start, reappearing perhaps five minutes later with the coffin and, we hoped, Peter inside it. At that moment it occurred to me to wonder who'd been in the first hearse since there was only one corpse in the 'dead room'. We had another crazy drive at top speed through the back streets of Hania, arriving at the cemetery fifteen minutes late, and finding the priest waiting on the steps of the chapel. Everything had been organized at such short notice that I was surprised by the amount of people who had turned up, and gratified that so many of them were Peter's Greek friends, several of whom helped Stavros carry the coffin into the chapel. The service started.

'Psst, psst!' I felt a tugging at my sleeve and, turning round, saw

222

the undertaker trying to catch my attention. 'Which grave is it?'

I had already shown him but I left the chapel and pointed it out again, coming back cringing at having interrupted the priest. He continued, and when the service was finished the coffin was carried solemnly to the graveside through the mud and rain and lowered on ropes. There was a muffled curse as someone slipped and it suddenly shot down dizzily while everybody sucked in their breaths with horror, expecting Peter to come hurtling out. At the last minute the rope was steadied with the faintest, but audible, titter of relief, and the coffin made its final descent before being sealed. As we went back to the cafeneion for Peter's farewell party, I hoped he had been watching the proceedings from some wine house in the Great Beyond. How he would have laughed! His funeral may not have gone according to plan, but it had turned out exactly as he would have wanted.